DAVID TRAHAIR

CPA, CA

THE PROCRASTINATOR'S GUIDE TO RETIREMENT

A CPA Canada Book

A Financial Guide to Retiring in Ten Years or Less

Cormorant Books

CPA   CHARTERED   COMPTABLES
      PROFESSIONAL   PROFESSIONNELS
      ACCOUNTANTS   AGRÉÉS
      CANADA   CANADA

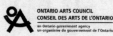

The publisher gratefully acknowledges the support of the Canada Council for the Arts and
the Ontario Arts Council for its publishing program. We acknowledge the financial support
of the Government of Canada through the Canada Book Fund (CBF) for our publishing
activities, and the Government of Ontario through Ontario Creates, an agency of the
Ontario Ministry of Culture, and the Ontario Book Publishing Tax Credit Program.

LIBRARY AND ARCHIVES CANADA CATALOGUING IN PUBLICATION

Title: The procrastinator's guide to retirement :
a financial guide to retiring in ten years or
less / David Trahair, CPA, CA.
Names: Trahair, David, author.
Description: A CPA Canada Book.
Identifiers: Canadiana (print) 20200341391 | Canadiana (ebook) 20200341413 |
ISBN 9781770866119 (softcover) | ISBN 9781770866126 (HTML)
Subjects: LCSH: Retirement—Canada—Planning. | LCSH: Finance, Personal—Canada.
Classification: LCC HQ1063.2.C2 T73 2021 | DDC 646.7/90971—dc23

Cover design: Angel Guerra / Archetype
Interior text design: Tannice Goddard / tannicegdesigns.ca
Printer: Friesens

Printed and bound in Canada.

CORMORANT BOOKS INC.
260 SPADINA AVENUE, SUITE 502, TORONTO, ON, M5T 2E4
www.cormorantbooks.com

*I would like to dedicate this book to my
ninety-one-year-old dad, Peter William Trahair.*

*Since I was born, he has been a shining example of how to live
your life. He has all the attributes: loving father, hard worker,
generous, and dedicated to the importance of healthy eating
and good exercise. To top it all off, he, along with my mom,
Florence, who passed away in 2008, gave me my "frugal gene."*

*Without his guidance, I would never have been in a position
to write a book like this.*

*Thanks, Dad.
With love, your son, David.*

Contents

INTRODUCTION   1

PART ONE / Ten Years or Less to Retirement

CHAPTER ONE: The Key: Tracking Your Current Spending   5

CHAPTER TWO: Your Golden Opportunity: When Expenses Decline   17

CHAPTER THREE: RRSP versus Paying Down the Mortgage   23

CHAPTER FOUR: The Procrastinator's Number Cruncher   33

CHAPTER FIVE: Your Pre-Retirement Investment Strategy   51

PART TWO / The Retirement Years

CHAPTER SIX: How Much Will You Spend During Retirement?   71

CHAPTER SEVEN: Maximizing Your Canada Pension Plan   81

CHAPTER EIGHT: Old Age Security: The Basics   91

CHAPTER NINE: Your Retirement Investment Strategy   95

CHAPTER TEN: Registered Retirement Income Fund versus Annuity   105

CHAPTER ELEVEN: Your Retirement Age   115

CHAPTER TWELVE: How Long Will You Live?   119

CHAPTER THIRTEEN: Old Age Health Care Planning   125

PART THREE / Special Situations

CHAPTER FOURTEEN: Attacking Debt   141

CHAPTER FIFTEEN: Your Home as a Source of Funds   153

CHAPTER SIXTEEN: Car Strategy: Lease or Buy?   159

CHAPTER SEVENTEEN: Planning for Elderly   169
   Parents and Inheritance

CHAPTER EIGHTEEN: Your Company Pension Plan   175

CHAPTER NINETEEN: Your Credit Card Strategy   183

CHAPTER TWENTY: The Financial Implications of Separation   193
   and Divorce

APPENDIX ONE: How to Track Your Spending   199

APPENDIX TWO: Estate Planning Record Keeper   206

GLOSSARY   207

ACKNOWLEDGEMENTS   213

ABOUT THE AUTHOR   215

Introduction

•

IF YOU AND YOUR SPOUSE are approaching retirement and have maximized your registered retirement savings plans (RRSPs), contributed the limit to your tax-free savings accounts (TFSAs), maintained no credit card or other consumer debt, paid off your mortgage, and perhaps even started saving outside your RRSPs and TFSAs, congratulations, you're all set for retirement!

If not, this book has been created for you, especially if you hope to retire in ten years or less and have the following concerns:

- There is just so much demand for our cash these days — the mortgage, car loan, house repairs, utilities, food, raising the kids, insurance, etc. — and we have a tough time just paying off our credit cards each month!
- Where do we get the thousands of dollars we are supposed to be putting into our RRSPs each year?
- We've thought about putting money in our TFSAs, but does that make sense if we are in debt?
- We have kids we hope will go to university. We know we can put up to $2,500 in a registered education savings plan (RESP) for

THE PROCRASTINATOR'S GUIDE TO RETIREMENT

each child in order to maximize the Canada Education Savings Grant, but where will that money come from?

- We're supposed to pay off the mortgage before retirement, but how is that possible?

For the vast majority of us, doing all those things is impossible. There just isn't enough money to do it all, so that means you will have to prioritize.

That is why I wrote this book — to show you how to do it. I will use knowledge gained from decades of studying personal finances, the four books I have already written on the subject, and feedback from the thousands of people who have taken my courses.

I'm going to guide you through the maze of retirement issues and point you in a clear direction to help you to live comfortably in your retirement.

This book is aimed at those who have less than ten years to go before retirement, i.e., those who are fifty-plus with a retirement plan that needs some work!

PART ONE

•

*Ten Years or Less
to Retirement*

CHAPTER ONE

The Key: Tracking Your Current Spending

•

THERE IS A RULE OF thumb that says you'll need 70 percent of your pre-retirement income to maintain your standard of living after you stop working. If only it were that simple!

The "70 percent rule" is problematic — it may be the right answer for one person but totally wrong for you because your financial situation is as individual as your fingerprints. Everyone is different, so relying on a simple rule of thumb is dangerous because you could end up saving too little (or even too much!). Relying on simple rules could end up devastating your retirement plans.

For many of you with a limited number of years left before you retire, the 70 percent rule may cause significant stress because saving enough to generate 70 percent of your income for a reasonable number of retirement years is going to be very difficult.

However, there is a simpler and more accurate way to determine how much you'll need to fund your retirement. It is easy to do and is perfectly customized to you. All you will need to do is spend a few hours following a step-by-step method to secure your financial future.

This book will show you how.

How Much Do You Spend?

It's very simple: to calculate how much you'll require to finance your retirement, you'll need to know how much you are going to spend during your retirement.

First, you need to know how much you spend now. Then you can make an objective projection of what you will spend during retirement. This is the problem with most of our retirement plans: we don't track our current spending, so we end up guessing about the future, and that is not a solid foundation upon which to build a retirement plan.

Once you start tracking your family's spending, it won't take very long to get an accurate picture of where all the money went. You'll need to invest a few hours a year, but it is the best way to ensure a comfortable retirement. Appendix 1 provides you with a step-by-step guide.

Meet Mike and Nancy Clark

To illustrate the strategies in this book, we will use a fictitious couple as an example: Mike and Nancy Clark.

- Mike is fifty-five, Nancy is fifty-three; they have a son, Joe, who is twenty-one and finishing his fourth year at university, and a daughter, Sophia, who is seventeen and is in grade twelve.
- Mike's gross salary is $80,000 a year and Nancy's is $50,000; both Joe and Sophia have part-time jobs.
- They own a home worth $400,000 with a $300,000 mortgage at the end of this year.
- The mortgage has twenty years of payments until it's paid off.
- They have one car, which is financed by a four-year loan.
- Their only savings are in their RRSPs: Mike's RRSP has a market value of $100,000 and Nancy's is $50,000 at the end of this year.
- They had a family RESP, but they used it all to finance Joe's education during his first three years of university.
- Mike and Nancy both hope to retire in ten years when Mike is sixty-five and Nancy is sixty-three.

The following table is a summary of their spending during the past year.

THE CLARKS' SPENDING		
	Cost	% of Total
Current Taxes and Withholdings		
CPP contributions	$5,121	4%
EI contributions	$1,670	1%
Income Tax	$24,650	19%
Sub-total	$31,441	24%
Automobile		
Auto fuel	$2,340	2%
Auto general	$350	0%
Auto insurance	$1,200	1%
Auto loan	$6,751	5%
Auto licence & registration	$180	0%
Auto repairs & maintenance	$400	0%
Sub-total	$11,221	8%
Children		
High school trips, lessons, etc.	$2,000	2%
University books, etc.	$1,200	1%
University meals & entertainment	$4,000	3%
University rent	$6,000	5%
University tuition	$6,400	5%
Sub-total	$19,600	15%
Family		
Cash withdrawals	$7,000	5%
Clothing	$4,000	3%

THE CLARKS' SPENDING		
	Cost	% of Total
Family cont.		
Donations	$300	0%
Entertainment	$900	1%
Groceries	$8,000	6%
Insurance (life, income protection)	$2,635	2%
Meals out	$3,500	3%
Medical & dental	$1,000	1%
Miscellaneous	$1,000	1%
Vacation	$6,000	5%
Sub-total	$34,335	26%
House		
House insurance	$1,200	1%
House repairs & maintenance	$2,900	2%
Mortgage	$21,753	16%
Phone & cable	$1,440	1%
Property tax	$3,500	3%
Security	$440	0%
Utilities (heat, hydro)	$3,510	3%
Sub-total	$34,743	26%
Interest and Bank Charges		
Bank charges	$120	0%
Credit card interest	$1,000	1%
	$1,120	1%
TOTAL EXPENSES	$132,460	100%
TOTAL GROSS INCOME	$130,000	
SHORTFALL	−$2,460	

This chart is what you need to create for your family — but first, let's review the Clarks' finances.

If you look at the bottom line (their income versus their spending), their gross salaries combined are $130,000, but they spent $132,460, so they spent $2,460 more than they made last year (and that is during a year in which they did not make any RRSP contributions).

Spending more than you make is easy: all you need is a credit card. The Clarks use credit cards and have built up a balance of $5,000 over the past few years, which they can't afford to pay off. As a result, they paid $1,000 in interest (at 20 percent) to the credit card company. If they continue spending like this for the next ten years until their retirement, the prognosis for their golden years is not good. Like most other Canadians, the ten years before they retire is going to be a key decade for the Clarks.

Many people are setting themselves up for failure because they don't track their spending. As a result, they don't realize their spending exceeds their income, so it will be very difficult for them to organize their finances before they retire.

But all is not lost. If you start planning now, a relaxing retirement is still possible.

For the Clarks, their priority has to be paying off their credit card balance, which means that they must target their expenses and reduce some of them so they can find the money to pay off the balance.

Focus on Expenses

Even though the list we just looked at has grouped the expenses, it can be a little overwhelming to try to analyze. If you use an Excel spreadsheet, it is easy to list and rearrange expense items. You need to focus on your biggest expenses to maximize your efforts to control them, so creating a list with your expenses arranged from largest to smallest will really help you.

Here is that list for the Clarks.

THE CLARKS' EXPENSES		
	Cost	% of Total
Income Tax	$24, 650	19%
Mortgage	$21,753	16%
Groceries	$8,000	6%
Cash withdrawals	$7,000	5%
Auto loan	$6,751	5%
University tuition	$6,400	5%
Vacation	$6,000	5%
University rent	$6,000	5%
CPP contributions	$5,121	4%
Clothing	$4,000	3%
University meals & entertainment	$4,000	3%
Utilities (heat, hydro)	$3,510	3%
Meals out	$3,500	3%
Property tax	$3,500	3%
House repairs & maintenance	$2,900	2%
Insurance (life, income protection)	$2,635	2%
Auto fuel	$2,340	2%
High school trips, lessons, etc.	$2,000	2%
EI contributions	$1,670	1%
Phone & cable	$1,440	1%
Auto insurance	$1,200	1%
House insurance	$1,200	1%
University books, etc.	$1,200	1%
Credit card interest	$1,000	1%

THE CLARKS' EXPENSES		
	Cost	% of Total
Medical & dental	$1,000	1%
Miscellaneous	$1,000	1%
Entertainment	$900	1%
Security	$440	0%
Auto repairs & maintenance	$400	0%
Auto general	$350	0%
Donations	$300	0%
Auto licence & registration	$180	0%
Bank charges	$120	0%
TOTAL EXPENSES	$132,460	100%

The results are interesting: income tax is by far the biggest expense, representing 19 percent of their total outflow.

The top ten items (income tax, mortgage, groceries, cash withdrawals, auto loan, university tuition, vacation, university rent, CPP contributions, and clothing) total $95,675, which is 72 percent of the total.

Their focus should be on which of the top ten they can eliminate or reduce. Let's look at each of them.

Income Tax

Since neither Mike nor Nancy is self-employed, there is not a lot of opportunity for them to split income with each other or their kids. Unfortunately, taxes are a necessity if we want to live in a civilized country, and there is not a lot the Clarks can do to significantly cut this amount. However, in later chapters we will see that there are important strategies they can employ that will ensure their tax bill is as low as possible during their retirement.

Mortgage

The Clarks are locked into a five-year mortgage, so there is not a lot they can do to reduce their mortgage payments at the moment. (See options for paying off your mortgage in Chapter 3.)

Groceries

Maybe they could cut the cost of their groceries, but everyone has to eat. Cutting this expense may lead to increased spending at restaurants and for takeout food. It may make sense for some people to spend *more* on groceries because, if the fridge is well stocked, they are less likely to pick up the phone to order takeout or go to a restaurant.

However, their son, Joe, will graduate from university this year, find a job, and move out, so he won't be eating at home. Their daughter, Sophia, is starting university in September, and the cost of her meals while at school is reflected under the category "university meals & entertainment." As a result, the Clarks' grocery bill is predicted to decline by $2,000 to $6,000 in the coming year.

Cash Withdrawals

The Clarks withdrew $7,000 in cash during the year and spent it. Where did all that money go?

Like most Canadians, they don't know. For many people, this is a huge opportunity to find where money is being wasted. One option for those who can handle credit is to use as little cash as possible. This means that you will have to pay using a credit or debit card, so the supplier's name will appear on your bank and credit card statements and you'll have a good idea of what the money was used for. (Note: This is a bad idea for people who can't handle credit, so if you have problems paying off your credit card, don't put more on the card to reduce your use of cash.)

It's possible that Mike and Nancy could save thousands of dollars each year if they became aware of where the money is going. Remember, you are more likely to change your spending behaviour if you track your money flow because you will be informed and motivated. Being financially healthy is a great motivator!

Mike and Nancy decide to track their cash spending and are success-ful in reducing it by $1,000, so their cash withdrawals are only $6,000 during the next year.

TIP

Another option is to get a cash-tracking app for your smart phone. I use one called CashTrails on my iPhone. This option is better than trying to keep receipts for every dime you spend. Simply enter the amount of cash you spend each day, select a category, and the app can email you a summary at the end of each month.

Auto Loan

As with the mortgage, they are locked into a four-year car loan, so there is not much they can do to reduce this expense now. (Note: As your car acquisition strategy is important for your retirement plans, in Chapter 16 we will discuss the benefits of buying versus leasing a car.)

University Tuition

Joe is in his fourth year at university, and his tuition fees for his last semester (from January to April) are $3,200. Sophia's tuition for her first semester (from September to December) is also $3,200, so the Clarks will be paying a total of $6,400 this year. Sophia's fees are esti-mated to grow by 2 percent to $6,528 next year, so there won't be an opportunity to reduce this expense.

Vacation

The Clarks spent $6,000 (5 percent of their total spending) on their vacation, a significant amount. Because they enjoy their annual vaca-tion with their kids, and there aren't going to be too many future opportunities for family vacations (Joe is graduating and moving out of the family home this year), the Clarks determine that they do not want to reduce this amount next year.

University Rent

Joe is living in a house with a few of his buddies while he is at university. His rent for the last four months is $3,000 ($750 a month). Sophia will be living in residence in September, and her costs are $3,000 for the term. Next year, Sophia's total costs are estimated to be $6,120.

TIP

Unfortunately, students who live in houses or apartments while at university usually have to pay rent for all twelve months of the year to ensure they have a place to stay for the eight months they are in school. This means that moving out of residence (where you pay for only eight months) to live in a house or apartment often doesn't result in any large savings.

Canada Pension Plan (CPP) Contributions

The Clarks can't avoid paying into their CPP plans since they earn salaries. The good news is that this is not really an expense. It is basically a forced retirement savings plan that for many people will be an important part of their retirement income. The Clarks can't do anything about this amount as it is determined by their incomes.

Clothing

This is a key discretionary expense. We need clothes, and most of us would like to wear the latest fashions, but is it really necessary for the Clarks to spend $4,000 each year? Mike and Nancy decide to stop and think before buying any new clothes and to make sure they look for bargains at the right time of year. They decide to reduce the amount spent by $1,000 in each of the next two years.

A Zero Credit Card Balance: Priceless

Having reviewed their expenses, in the next year the Clarks aim to:

- spend $2,000 less on groceries,

- save $1,000 in reduced cash withdrawals,
- reduce their clothing expenses by $1,000, and
- save $2,000 on Sophia's high school trips and lessons (since she is going to university).

Thus, they will reduce their spending by $6,000 next year, resulting in an excess cash flow of $3,928. That amount can go directly to paying down their credit card balance from $5,000 to $1,072, so they will have no credit card debt at the end of the following year.

Note that the Clarks' credit card balance is fairly low in relation to their incomes, so they are in relatively good shape financially. Unfortunately, many Canadians are carrying a large amount of consumer debt, which is a major problem when incomes decline, as they have discovered with the onset of the COVID-19 crisis.

Over the past few years, the balances on credit cards and lines of credit that Canadians carry have grown at an alarming rate, so Chapter 14 is dedicated to eliminating debt.

CHAPTER TWO

Your Golden Opportunity: When Expenses Decline

•

DURING THE NEXT YEAR, THE Clarks will have one focus: to get rid of their credit card balance. They need to forget saving for retirement, forget trying to pay down the mortgage, forget TFSA contributions. But what about the remaining years until their retirement? From a financial point of view, the last nine years before they retire are going to be the most important of their lives. This is the make-or-break period for their retirement plans.

The following chart on the next page shows a projection of their spending during Years 1 through 10.

Please note that in this chart we have made the following assumptions:

- Inflation is estimated to be 2 percent per year.
- Mike and Nancy's salaries grow at 1 percent per year.
- Estimated income tax, CPP, and EI withholdings are at 2019 Ontario rates.
- Most expenses increase at the rate of inflation, except for the auto loan and mortgage (which are based on the loan rates and terms) and discretionary items (including cash withdrawals, clothing, donations, entertainment, interest, and bank charges that depend on debt balances).

THE CLARKS' ANNUAL EXPENSES
(Current Inflation 2 percent)

	Year 0	Year 1	Year 2	Year 3	Year 4	Year 5	Year 6	Year 7	Year 8	Year 9	Year 10
Mike's Age	55	56	57	58	59	60	61	62	63	64	65
Taxes and withholdings	$31,441	$31,868	$32,298	$32,735	$33,174	$33,620	$34,067	$34,513	$34,966	$35,420	$35,892
Auto	$11,221	$11,311	$11,402	$11,495	$4,838	$5,495	$6,085	$3,707	$11,922	$12,025	$12,130
Children	$19,600	$17,952	$18,311	$18,677	$9,525	$0	$0	$0	$0	$0	$0
Family	$34,335	$30,618	$30,905	$32,200	$32,499	$29,182	$29,361	$29,545	$29,732	$29,922	$30,117
House	$34,743	$35,003	$35,267	$35,537	$35,813	$36,095	$36,382	$36,674	$36,973	$37,277	$37,588
Interest and bank charges	$1,120	$620	$120	$120	$120	$120	$120	$120	$120	$120	$120
Total Expenses	$132,460	$127,372	$128,303	$130,764	$115,969	$104,512	$106,015	$104,559	$113,713	$114,764	$115,847
Combined Gross Salaries	$130,000	$131,300	$132,613	$133,939	$135,278	$136,631	$137,997	$139,377	$140,771	$142,179	$143,601
Excess Income	−$2,460	$3,928	$4,310	$3,175	$19,309	$32,119	$31,982	$34,818	$27,058	$27,415	$27,754

For a more detailed version of this spreadsheet, please see www.trahair.com or cpacanada.ca/retirement.

Attack Credit Card Debt First

During Year 1, the excess income the Clarks have is $3,928. This is much better than the $2,460 shortfall they had last year, and the entire amount is used to pay down the $5,000 credit card balance to $1,072.

In Year 2, the excess is $4,310, and $1,072 of that is used to pay off the credit card balance. The remaining $3,238 is put into the Clarks' bank account.

The Golden Opportunity Years

In Year 3, the excess is $3,175. This excess also goes into their bank account.

Then some really good news: in Year 4, the surplus rises to $19,309, and during Years 5 through 10, the surpluses are greater than $27,000 each year. In fact, the total excess money they will have during Years 4 to 10 will be an astounding $200,455. How did this amazing development happen? Let's look at the details.

First of all, their salaries will increase each year by 1 percent. Their combined gross salaries go from $135,278 in Year 4 to $143,601 in Year 10. After taking off income tax, CPP, and EI, their net pay has gone from $102,104 to $107,709 during the same period. That's an increase of $5,605.

Why did the excess in Year 4 increase so much? One reason is because the Clarks paid off the car loan that had cost $6,751 each year. Then they had four years with a paid-off car and had to cover only the operating costs, repairs, and maintenance. It is assumed they sold their old car for $2,500 and bought another similar car in Year 8 and again started annual payments of $6,751.

But the really big increase in the excess income is during Year 5. That is when their daughter, Sophia, graduates from university. Spending on her education will go from $18,677 in Year 3 to $9,525 in Year 4 to zero in Year 5. If you have children in university, the year they graduate will probably have a significant positive impact on your personal finances.

But there are other savings as well. Hopefully, in Year 5 Sophia will be earning her own money, so Mike and Nancy's spending on her will go down (even if she moves back home for a few years). We therefore estimate that cash withdrawals, clothing, and grocery costs will each decline by $1,000 per year starting in Year 5.

Years 2 through 10 are the golden opportunity years for the Clarks. What they do with the excess money earned during these years will make or break their retirement plans. If they simply increase their spending, they are dooming their future. If they spend it all, they will be sentencing themselves to watching every penny for the rest of their lives. You don't want that to happen to you!

Dealing with Excess Funds

What should the Clarks do with the extra funds? They have three main options:

- Make RRSP contributions;
- Pay down the mortgage;
- Make TFSA contributions.

Let's look at a TFSA as an option versus an RRSP.

Tax-Free Savings Account

The TFSA was introduced in 2009 for Canadian residents aged eighteen years and older. From 2009 to 2012, you could contribute up to $5,000 to your TFSA. In 2013 and 2014, the annual amount was $5,500 per year; in 2015, it was raised to $10,000; from 2016 to 2018, it was $5,500; and for 2019 and 2020, it was $6,000. If you have not made any contributions prior to 2020, your TFSA room is $69,500.

TFSA TIPS

- Contributions and interest on any money borrowed to invest in TFSAs are not tax-deductible. All income generated is tax-free, even when amounts are withdrawn from your TFSA.

- If you withdraw an amount from your TFSA in a calendar year, the amount you withdraw is added to your contribution room the next calendar year.

TFSA TRAP

Remember that if you transfer an existing investment from a regular taxable investment account to a TFSA, there is a "deemed disposition." In other words, you are deemed to have sold the investment upon the transfer, even though you didn't, so you could end up having to declare and pay tax on any capital gain if the investment you are transferring is worth more than you paid for it. Also, if the stock is worth less, you are not allowed to take a capital loss on the transfer.

TFSA or RRSP?

Whether it is best to invest in a TFSA or an RRSP (where you get a tax deduction) generally depends on your tax situation. If you are in a medium-to-high tax bracket when you make an RRSP contribution and a lower tax bracket when you withdraw the RRSP funds (and pay tax on the withdrawal), RRSPs are usually the better option.

On the other hand, if you are in your twenties and in a low tax bracket, and you will be in a higher tax bracket when you withdraw the funds (e.g., in retirement), a TFSA usually makes more sense than an RRSP.

In the Clarks' case, Mike makes $80,000 per year and Nancy makes $50,000. Here are their marginal tax rates in each province in 2020.

MARGINAL TAX RATES		
	Mike	Nancy
Alberta	30.5%	30.5%
British Columbia	28.2%	28.2%

MARGINAL TAX RATES		
	Mike	**Nancy**
Manitoba	37.9%	33.25%
New Brunswick	35.32%	35.32%
Newfoundland and Labrador	36.3%	35%
Nova Scotia	37.17%	35.98%
Northwest Territories	29.1%	29.1%
Nunavut	27.5%	27.5%
Ontario	31.48%	29.65%
Prince Edward Island	37.2%	34.3%
Quebec	37.12%	37.12%
Saskatchewan	33%	33%
Yukon	29.5%	29.5%

Later, we will see that the Clarks are both going to be in lower tax brackets after they retire, so the RRSP seems to be the better option for them.

The next question is: contribute to their RRSPs or pay down the mortgage?

This is a more complex question, so we will look at it in Chapter 3.

CHAPTER THREE

RRSP versus Paying Down the Mortgage

•

IF YOU HAVE EXTRA CASH to invest, choosing to invest in your RRSP or pay down your mortgage are both good options. However, if you have other consumer debt, such as a credit card balance, you need to consider paying it off before you make a decision regarding your RRSP versus your mortgage. It all depends on your personal situation, so we'll look at that now.

What Debt Do You Have?

The question never seems to be "Should I contribute to my RRSP or pay down my credit card debt, which is charging me 20 percent interest per year?" That's because the answer to that question is obvious — anyone with a revolving credit card balance at a high rate of interest should not be making RRSP contributions. You are never going to consistently beat a 20 percent annual rate of return after taxes and fees by investing in any portfolio today. But you would get that rate of return simply by getting rid of your debt.

How can you get a rate of return by paying off debt? It's simple: a lack of cash outflow is as good as a cash inflow, and better if that inflow is taxed. Let's look at an example to explain this.

You have a credit card balance of $10,000, which you can't afford to pay off in full. If the interest rate is 20 percent, you'll have to pay $2,000 in interest in one year. If you had an investment of $10,000, it would need to generate a return of greater than 20 percent for you to break even because you'd have to pay tax on the income and be left with $2,000 after tax.

For example, if you were in a 30 percent marginal tax bracket (for each additional dollar you made, you'd have to pay $0.30 in tax) and you had an investment of $10,000, you would need to generate income of $2,857 (a return of 28.6 percent) just to break even. That's because you'd have to pay 30 percent tax on the income of $2,857, which is $857, leaving you with $2,000. How likely are you to find something that is going to pay you that kind of return? Not very likely.

So by paying off the credit card, you achieve an after-tax rate of return of 20 percent, which in this case is equivalent to achieving a 28.6 percent rate of return before tax on an investment.

TIP

Anyone with credit card debt at a rate of 20 percent or higher should call their credit card issuer immediately and switch to a basic card without all the bells, whistles, and points. This simple move will probably save you 10 percent or more in reduced rates. Better still, shop around for the best rate. Many competing financial institutions offer balance transfer options at low, or sometimes even zero, rates. We'll discuss this in more detail in Chapter 19.

If You Only Have a Mortgage

When we ask ourselves the question "Should I contribute to my RRSP or pay down the mortgage?" we assume there is no ugly high-interest debt, only a mortgage. This is the position the Clarks would be in after they paid off their $5,000 credit card balance. What should they do?

The commonsensical answer is to make the RRSP contribution and use the tax refund to pay down the mortgage. This sounds like a great idea, as you get the best of both worlds, but it's not really as simple as that.

I have created a spreadsheet called the RRSP vs Pay Down Debt Calculator. It is a Microsoft Excel spreadsheet where you can enter the variables in your own personal situation to determine the optimal solution. (You can download it free from my website at www.trahair.com or at cpacanada.ca/retirement).

Let's use a simple example to illustrate how to use it.

- You have a mortgage with a balance greater than $10,000 and you are allowed to pay it down by $10,000.
- You have $10,000 cash available, and you are in a 35 percent marginal tax bracket now as well as when you cash in your RRSP.
- Assume a 4 percent rate of return after fees on your RRSP and a 4 percent effective annual rate on the mortgage.
- Focus on a ten-year period, as we have been doing for the Clarks.

One option is to pay down the mortgage with your $10,000 available cash. If you did this, you would have nothing in your RRSP and $10,000 less on your mortgage for the ten-year period.

The alternative is to make a $10,000 RRSP contribution and, with the income tax refund of $3,500, pay down the mortgage by that amount.

In ten years, your $10,000 RRSP will grow at 4 percent, compounded annually, to $14,802. You then withdraw the money and pay tax at the 35 percent marginal tax rate. That leaves you with $9,622 cash in hand.

So what happened to the mortgage? It grew at 4 percent per year compounded annually over the ten-year period. After ten years, the $6,500 still owing on the mortgage ($10,000 less the $3,500 tax refund you paid it down by) grew to $9,622, which is the $6,500 plus $3,122 of accumulated interest.

If you used the $9,622 cash in hand from cashing in your RRSP to pay off the mortgage, you would be in the exact same position as if you had simply paid off the mortgage in the first year.

RRSP VERSUS PAYING DOWN DEBT

Cash available	$10,000
Personal marginal income tax rate now	35%
Personal marginal income tax rate on withdrawal	35%
Interest rate on debt	4%
Annual growth rate of RRSP	4%

RRSP	Year 1	Year 2	Year 3	Year 4	Year 5	Year 6	Year 7	Year 8	Year 9	Year 10
Ending RRSP Value	$10,400	$10,816	$11,249	$11,699	$12,167	$12,653	$13,159	$13,686	$14,233	$14,802

RRSP withdrawal	$14,802
Tax on RRSP withdrawal	-$5,180
After-tax funds on RRSP withdrawal	$9,622

DEBT	Year 1	Year 2	Year 3	Year 4	Year 5	Year 6	Year 7	Year 8	Year 9	Year 10
Cumulative Interest on Debt	$260	$530	$812	$1,104	$1,408	$1,725	$2,054	$2,396	$2,752	$14,802

Total interest accrued in a ten-year period	$3,122
Original principal of loan that needs to be paid	$6,500
Balance of debt after ten-year period	$9,622
Excess (or Shortfall) of RRSP vs Debt	$0

Key Variable: Marginal Tax Rates

Here is the key point: the example we just went through assumes the marginal tax rate remains the same during the ten-year period and that the RRSP grows at the same rate as the interest rate on the mortgage.

Under this scenario, the answer to the question comes down to whether you think the after-fee rate of return on your RRSP investments is going to beat the rate of interest on your mortgage. If the marginal tax rate is lower when the RRSP withdrawal is made, the RRSP wins. If the marginal rate is higher upon withdrawal, paying down the mortgage wins.

In our example, if your marginal tax rate is 46 percent now and only 35 percent when you withdraw your RRSP, the RRSP option wins by $1,628. If the situation is reversed and your marginal rate is 35 percent now and 46 percent upon withdrawal, the mortgage payment wins by the exact same amount.

For most people, their marginal tax rate will be lower when they withdraw from their RRSP, so the RRSP is often the best option — at least, it looks that way on paper.

Say your marginal tax rate is 45 percent at the time of the RRSP contribution and 35 percent upon withdrawal ten years later. If the mortgage interest rate was 4 percent, the RRSP annual rate of return required would be only 2.28 percent. That is because the higher initial tax refund that was used to pay down the mortgage means the RRSP does not need to grow to as high an amount to pay off the mortgage at the end.

Beyond the Numbers

Reducing personal financial decisions to numbers on a spreadsheet is always a good start. But you have to dig deeper in your financial decisions because human nature can have a powerful impact. Often, other factors outweigh what the numbers show. Let me explain.

There are several advantages to opting to pay down the mortgage instead of making RRSP contributions that aren't clear when looking at a simple spreadsheet.

Rate of Return

First of all, the rate of return on the mortgage is guaranteed. You know what return you are going to make because the interest rate is set. With an RRSP, your rate of return is unknown. Your investments might do well, but in today's environment, how confident can you be about that?

That's the problem with the spreadsheet: it's easy to optimistically insert a great rate of return that you hope you'll get, but if you don't actually make it, you've made a decision based on a false assumption.

Marginal Tax Rates

This is less of an issue because most people will be in a lower tax bracket when they retire, but that may not be your case. For example, you may be unfortunate enough to be laid off and have to access your RRSP in a year when you still have significant taxable income before you retire. That's when RRSPs don't work so well for you.

Will You Ever Pay Off Your Mortgage?

This is perhaps the most important reason for prioritizing debt reduction ahead of RRSP investing. If you convince yourself that your RRSP is going to do very well, it takes the pressure off paying down your mortgage. In other words, if you decide the RRSP is the better option, you tend to reduce the importance of paying off your mortgage.

You may worry less about getting a home equity line of credit to finance a home renovation, for example. You may even decide to extend your mortgage amortization period (the time to pay it off), and you may be less concerned about retiring with a mortgage.

If you rank paying down your mortgage ahead of your RRSP, you'll be much more focused on reducing the balance and much more likely to pay it off before you retire.

Paying off your mortgage essentially forces you to be fiscally prudent. It makes you live within your means and spend less than you make because you can't pay down your mortgage if you have no money!

Carrying a Mortgage into Retirement

Putting RRSP contributions ahead of paying down the mortgage means that you are choosing to carry the mortgage for a longer period of time. If you can afford to make RRSP contributions and are on schedule to pay off your mortgage by retirement, you're fine. Don't change a thing.

If, however, you are planning to go into retirement with a mortgage, I'd like you to spend a few minutes thinking about the consequences. You are choosing to shackle yourself with monthly payments after your income has declined. How are you going to pay those amounts on a lower fixed retirement income? It will probably be very stressful, to say the least.

We'll get into all the different sources of your retirement income in Part 2 of this book, but effectively you'll need to have saved more money in your RRSP in order to pay your mortgage.

Let's look at how much more you'll need.

For example, say you have just retired and you have a $200,000 balance on your mortgage. Your mortgage is at 4 percent interest per year and has ten years remaining until it is paid off. Your monthly mortgage payments are $2,021.77.

If you were in the 35 percent marginal tax bracket after retirement, your RRSP would have to pay out $3,110.42 per month so you'd have enough left to pay the mortgage. In other words, tax of $1,088.65 (35 percent of $3,110.42) would need to be paid, leaving $2,021.77 each month to pay the mortgage.

How large an RRSP would you need at retirement to pay out $3,110.42 a month for ten years? Assuming the RRSP grows at 5 percent a year from retirement for each of the ten years, the answer is $293,254.75.

So, if you went into retirement with a $200,000 mortgage, you'd need $293,254.75 extra in your RRSP just to break even. And that assumes you continue to make 5 percent after fees on your RRSP for the next ten years.

Put another way, you'd be just as well off as someone who had a zero mortgage balance and $293,254.75 less in their RRSP.

I have created another spreadsheet for you to use to do your own calculations. It's called the RRSP Needed for Mortgage Calculator. (You can download it free from my website at www.trahair.com or at cpacanada.ca/retirement.)

Here is what the calculator has come up with for a range of options:

Summary Examples	1	2	3	4	5	6
Original mortgage balance	$200,000	$200,000	$200,000	$200,000	$200,000	$200,000
Annual interest rate	4%	4%	4%	4%	4%	5%
Term (years)	10	15	10	10	10	10
Marginal tax bracket	35%	35%	35%	25%	45%	40%
Monthly payment (calculated)	$2,021.77	$1,476.08	$2,021.77	$2,021.77	$2,021.77	$2,116.30
RRSP monthly pre-tax amount needed	$3,110,42	$2,270.89	$3,110.42	$2,695.70	$3,675.95	$3,527.16
RRSP needed at retirement	$293,254.75	$287,165.74	$322,120.71	$254,154.11	$363,074.50	$365,279.34

You will notice that the size of the RRSP needed in each example moves in step with marginal tax rates. It increases as the marginal tax rate increases and decreases when it declines.

The RRSP needed, however, relates inversely to the rate of return your RRSP generates. As the rate of return on the RRSP decreases, the size of the RRSP needed increases, and vice versa.

Look at example #5 on the chart. If the marginal tax rate is 45 percent and the RRSP's annual rate of return is only 4 percent, the RRSP balance needed going into retirement would be $363,074.50, fully $69,819.75 higher than the first example.

What Should the Clarks Do?

Let's have a look at the RRSP versus paying down the mortgage decision for the Clarks.

You'll recall that we looked at their spending in relation to their income over a ten-year period, and we found they made significant progress and had large cash surpluses in Years 4 through 10. To decide which option is best for them, we have to look at their financial situation at the beginning of the ten-year period compared to their situation at the end. That means we need to look at their net worth statement, i.e., their personal financial scorecard. The net worth statement summarizes their assets and their liabilities.

We will assume the following for the Clarks at the start of Year 1:

- They have nothing in the bank.
- Their house is worth $400,000.
- Their mortgage balance is $300,000 with twenty years left, and they are paying 4 percent interest.
- Their house will appreciate at 2 percent per year.
- They have $5,000 of credit card debt.
- Their credit card interest rate is 20 percent per year.
- Mike's RRSP is worth $100,000 and Nancy's is worth $50,000.
- Their RRSPs will grow at 4 percent per year.

Here is what the Clarks' net worth statement looks like at the start of Year 1 and at the end of Year 10 if they only put the excess cash in a bank account:

	Start of Year 1	End of Year 10
Assets		
Bank	$0	$206,868
House	$400,000	$487,598
RRSP — Mike	$100,000	$148,024
RRSP — Nancy	$50,000	$74,012
Total Assets	$550,000	$916,502
Liabilities		
Mortgage	$300,000	$179,322
Credit card	$5,000	$0
Total liabilities	$305,000	$179,322
Net Worth	$245,000	$737,180

Their net worth has gone up significantly, from $245,000 to $737,180. That's an increase of $492,180, a significant amount. But this assumes the excess money they earn each year is put in a bank account that earns no interest. That would not be a good investment. The Clarks have two main options: make RRSP contributions or pay down the mortgage.

There are many variables that affect the calculation, so I have created a spreadsheet that you can use for your personal calculations. We'll look at it in Chapter 4.

CHAPTER FOUR

The Procrastinator's Number Cruncher

•

IT IS VERY UNLIKELY THAT your financial situation is exactly the same as that of the Clarks, so I have created a customized spreadsheet to help you: the Procrastinator's Number Cruncher. You can download it free at www.trahair.com or at cpacanada.ca/retirement.

The Procrastinator's Number Cruncher

When you open the spreadsheet, you'll see the following tabs at the bottom of the page:

- Home
- Questions
- Detailed Results
- Summary Results
- Tax Info
- Assumptions

Home

The "Home" tab gives you some information about the spreadsheet and provides the version number (the date that the spreadsheet was last updated).

Questions

This is the place for you to answer specific questions about your personal situation. The spreadsheet needs to know a lot about you and your spouse or common-law partner before it can perform the calculations to help you optimize your retirement situation.

Here are the questions you'll need to answer for each of you:

General

- What is today's date?
- What is your first name?
- What is your last name?
- On what day were you born?
- In what province/territory do you reside?

Income/Expenses

- What is your current total income before expenses from salary?
- If you wish your salary to increase, enter the annual rate; if not, enter 0.
- What is your current net income from self-employment?
- If you wish your self-employment earnings to increase, enter the annual rate; if not, enter 0.
- What percentage of your self-employment earnings (if any) could you split with your spouse?
- What net rental income (loss) do you expect this year?
- Enter the annual rate you expect your rental income to grow by.
- What actual amount of ineligible dividends do you expect this year?
- Enter the annual rate you expect your ineligible dividends to grow by.

Spending

- How much will you spend in the current year on everything other than your mortgage? (This is a key question, so if you have not already tracked your spending for last year — see directions in Chapter 1, Chapter 14, and Appendix 1 — take the time to do it now.)
- At what rate do you want your spending to increase each year? If zero, enter 0?
- What percentage of your spending (excluding mortgage) in your final working year will you need after retirement?

Pensions/Other

- Do you have a pension plan at work?
- What is your pension contribution rate (percentage of salary you must contribute)?
- How much money do you expect from your pension the first year of retirement?
- At what age will your pension start?
- If your pension is indexed to inflation, enter inflation rate; if not, enter 0.
- How much money (before tax) from other sources in today's dollars do you expect to earn each year after you retire (e.g., part-time consulting work)?
- At what age do you expect this income from other sources to stop?
- What average annual rate of inflation do you expect over the remainder of your life?
- Would you like to split your pension income with your spouse?

Investments

- What percentage would you like to allocate to each of the four options?
- — RRSP
- — TFSA

— Investment

— Mortgage

(Note: Total must be 100 percent.)

RRSP/RRIF

- What was the total market value of your RRSP/RRIF on the most recent statement?
- How much do you plan to contribute to your RRSP this first year?
- What is your opening RRSP room carried forward from prior years?
- At what age do you plan to retire and stop making RRSP contributions?
- Would you like to make spousal RRSP contributions?
- What percent of your RRSP contributions do you want to make spousal?
- At what annual rate do you expect your RRSP/RRIF investments to grow until you retire?
- At what annual rate do you expect your RRSP/RRIF investments to grow after you retire?

TFSA

- What is the current value of your TFSA?
- How much do you plan to contribute to your TFSA this first year?
- How much can you contribute to your TFSA at the start?
- How much can you and your spouse contribute to a TFSA each year?
- At what annual rate do you expect your TFSA to increase?

Regular Investment Account

- What is the current value of your investment account?
- What amount of taxable eligible dividends will you earn this first year?
- What amount of interest will you earn this first year?
- What is the mix of investments in your regular investment account

(outside your RRSP/TFSA) (% equity)?

- What average dividend yield do you expect on your equities in your investment account?
- At what annual rate do you think your regular investments outside your RRSP/TFSA will increase by?
- What interest rate do you think your fixed income investments will pay?

Principal Residence

- What is the current market value of your principal residence if you own one?
- At what rate do you expect the value of your house to increase by each year?
- What is the current balance on your mortgage?
- How much extra do you plan to pay down your mortgage by this first year?
- What is the interest rate on your mortgage?
- What amortization period is your mortgage (i.e., the number of years left)?

Old Age Security

- Are you eligible for the maximum Old Age Security (OAS) pension? (If you have lived in Canada for at least forty years after turning eighteen, you will receive the maximum pension.)
- If not, how many years will you have lived in Canada since your eighteenth birthday when you turn sixty-five? (You must have lived in Canada for at least ten years to qualify for OAS.)
- At what age would you like to start receiving your OAS pension? (Enter an age between sixty-five and seventy. It will be increased by 7.2 percent for each year after age sixty-five.)

Canada Pension Plan

- Are you eligible for the maximum Canada Pension Plan (CPP) pension at age sixty-five? (If, on average, from age eighteen to retirement your earnings exceeded the maximum pensionable earnings — $57,400 in 2019 — you should receive the maximum CPP pension.)

- If not, what has your average annual income from earnings been since you turned eighteen? (Enter a figure between $0 and $57,400.)
- At what age would you like to start receiving your CPP pension? (Enter an age between sixty and seventy. It will be reduced by 7.2 percent for each year before age sixty-five and increased by 8.4 percent for each year after age sixty-five.)
- Would you like to split your CPP pension income with your spouse?

Longevity

- Until what age do you think you will live?

The Clarks Use the Number Cruncher

We are going to use the spreadsheet to see what the best option is for the Clarks, i.e., whether to make RRSP contributions or to pay down their mortgage during the final ten years before they retire.

Here are the key answers to the questions for the Clarks:

	Mike	Nancy
General		
Date of birth	1964-04-24	1966-04-13
In what province/territory do you reside?	Ontario	Ontario
Income/Expenses		
What is your current total income before expenses from salary?	$80,800	$50,500
If you wish your salary to increase, enter the annual rate, if not, enter 0.	1%	1%
Spending		
How much will you spend in the current year on everything other than your mortgage?	$0	$77,679

	Mike	Nancy
At what rate do you want your spending to increase each year, if zero, enter 0.	1%	1%
What percentage of your spending (excluding mortgage) in your final working year will you need after retirement?	60%	60%
Pensions/Other		
Do you have a pension plan at work?	N	N
How much money (before tax) from other sources in today's dollars do you expect each year after you retire?	$0	$0
Investments		
What percentage would you like to allocate to each of the four options?		
RRSP	100%	100%
TFSA	0%	0%
Investment	0%	0%
Mortgage	0%	0%
RRSP/RRIF		
What was the total market value of your RRSP/RRIF on the most recent statement?	$100,000	$50,000
How much do you plan to contribute to your RRSP this first year?	$0	$0
What is your opening RRSP room carried forward from prior years?	$200,000	$50,000
At what age do you plan to retire and stop making RRSP contributions?	65	63
What percent of your RRSP contributions do you want to make spousal?	0%	0%
At what annual rate do you expect your RRSP/RRIF investments to grow until you retire?	5%	5%
At what annual rate do you expect your RRSP/RRIF investments to grow after you retire?	4%	4%
TFSA		
What is the current value of your TFSA?	$0	$0

	Mike	Nancy
How much do you plan to contribute to your TFSA this first year?	$0	$0
How much can you contribute to a TFSA at the start?	$69,500	$69,500
How much can you and your spouse contribute to a TFSA each year?	$6,000	$6,000
At what annual rate do you think your TFSA will increase by?	4%	4%
Regular Investment Account		
What is the opening value of your investment account?	$0	$0
Principal Residence		
What is the current market value of your principal residence if you own one?	$400,000	$0
At what rate do you expect the value of your house to increase by per year?	2%	N/A
What is the current balance on your mortgage?	$300,000	N/A
How much extra do you plan to pay down your mortgage by this first year?	$0	N/A
What is the interest rate on your mortgage?	4%	N/A
What amortization period is your mortgage (i.e., the number of years left)?	20	N/A
Old Age Security		
Are you eligible for the maximum Old Age Security OAS pension at age 65?	Y	Y
If not, how many years will you have lived in Canada since your 18th birthday when you turn 65?	N/A	N/A
At what age would you like to start receiving your OAS pension? (Enter an age between 65 and 70.)	65	65
Canada Pension Plan		
Are you eligible for the maximum Canada Pension Plan (CPP) pension at age 65?	Y	N

	Mike	Nancy
If not, what has your average annual income from earnings been since you turned 18? (Enter a figure between $0 and $57,400.)	N/A	$50,500
At what age would you like to start receiving your CPP pension? (Enter an age between 60 and 70.)	65	65
Would you like to split your CPP income with your spouse?	N	N
Longevity		
What age do you think you will live until?	85	85

There are a few things to note before we get started.

Retirement Age

The Clarks want to retire in the same year, when Mike is sixty-five and Nancy is sixty-three.

Spending

You'll note that the amount the Clarks spend in the current year on everything other than the mortgage is in Nancy's column. That is because this forces the program to leave any excess funds that the family has to Mike's side because he is the one in the higher tax bracket, so it makes more sense for him to make RRSP contributions rather than Nancy.

The total spending excludes the mortgage because the spreadsheet calculates and tracks your mortgage for you.

As we saw in the chart in Chapter 2, the Clarks' total spending in Year 1 was $127,372. Deduct $21,753 for the mortgage payments and $31,868 for taxes, CPP, and EI, and they are left with $73,751.

Why does the chart show a total of $77,679? The excess $3,928 is added to the total because the Clarks are going to use that amount to pay down the credit card balance, which reduces the amount available to either pay down the mortgage or make an RRSP contribution.

Allocation of Excess Funds

You may also note that we have allocated the excess 100 percent to the RRSP and 0 percent to the mortgage as a starting point. We will then reverse this allocation to see which is the better option.

Note that the program's logic is to try to conform to the allocation you enter on the "Questions" tab. However, it may not be possible.

For example, if you try to allocate an amount to your RRSP that is over your allowable RRSP limit, it won't let you. Similarly, the program can't allocate the excess to pay down the mortgage once you have paid the mortgage off.

Once you have paid off the mortgage, the program will allocate any excess funds to your RRSP. If there are still any excess funds, it will first allocate them to your TFSA (up to your allowable limits); once you are maxed out on your TFSA, the rest will go to your regular investment account. This ranking makes sense because why would you put money in a regular taxable investment account when you could put the funds in a TFSA instead and shelter all earnings from tax?

If you choose the RRSP option and you max out your RRSP contributions, the program will allocate any excess funds to your TFSA first and then to your investment account. If you would prefer to allocate the excess to paying down your mortgage, you'll need to override the allocation to do this. This is simple to do, as the program allows you to change the allocations on the Detailed Results tab each year. In fact, you can override any number on the Detailed Results tab.

Note that since Nancy does not have the mortgage, I have allocated 100 percent to her RRSP. But since the program allocates any shortfall in one spouse's column to the other spouse, Nancy won't have any excess to deal with (i.e., we are forcing the excess onto Mike's side by allocating all of Nancy's excess spending against his after-tax salary).

With the 100 percent RRSP option, it would take nineteen more years to pay off the mortgage. Mike and Nancy would not be mortgage-free until Mike is seventy-five, which means they would be saddled with annual mortgage payments of $21,753 for nine years of their retirement.

If 100 percent of the excess was allocated to paying down the mortgage, it would only take nine years to pay off the mortgage, so the

Clarks would be mortgage-free one year before their retirement, when Mike is sixty-four.

The Three Options

Using three options, the following is a summary of the values at the end of Year 10, which Mike and Nancy will reach at their respective retirement ages of sixty-five and sixty-three:

	Option 1 Excess Money in Bank End of Year 10	Option 2 100% RRSP End of Year 10	Option 3 100% Pay Down Mortgage End of Year 10
Assets			
Bank	$206,868	$0	$0
House	$487,598	$487,598	$487,598
RRSP — Mike	$148,024	$503,800	$231,085
RRSP — Nancy	$74,012	$81,445	$81,445
Total Assets	$916,502	$1,072,843	$800,128
Liabilities			
Mortgage	$179,322	$179,322	$0
Total liabilities	$179,322	$179,322	$0
Net Worth	$737,180	$893,521	$800,128

At Mike's retirement age of sixty-five, this comparison shows the RRSP option wins by $93,393 with a total net worth of $893,521, versus only $800,128 for the pay down the mortgage option. However, this is essentially comparing apples to oranges for one key reason: tax.

Be Careful of Tax

The RRSP investments are shown at their pre-tax values, so tax would have to be paid to cash them in. Therefore, the higher RRSP value in

43

THE PROCRASTINATOR'S GUIDE TO RETIREMENT

the middle column for Mike's RRSP is not really comparable because it doesn't show the taxes that would have to be paid when it is cashed in.

Consider Cash Flow Implications

The other important issue is the future cash flows of the various options. The 100 percent RRSP option still has a mortgage balance of $179,322, which carries with it the requirement to continue paying annual mortgage payments of $21,753 for the next ten years until Mike is seventy-five.

Which Option Wins?

In the final analysis, the RRSP option has resulted in Mike's RRSP having a value of $503,800 with a mortgage balance of $179,322, while the pay down the mortgage option has resulted in Mike's RRSP having a value of $231,085 with no mortgage.

Is the extra $272,715 in Mike's RRSP enough to make up for the balance still owing on the mortgage?

With a balance of $179,322 and monthly payments of $1,813, it will take ten years to pay the mortgage off, which is 120 monthly payments. If Mike was in a 30 percent income tax bracket when he retired, monthly RRSP income amounts of $2,590 would be required to make the monthly mortgage payment (30 percent tax on $2,590 is $777, leaving $1,813 to pay the mortgage).

Assuming the RRSP was making a return of 4 percent throughout the 120 months, in order to pay off the mortgage an opening balance of $255,778 in the RRSP would be required to pay out $16,937 a month for ten years. Mike's RRSP is $272,715 higher in option 2, so it seems the 100 percent RRSP option wins by $16,937 on a before-tax basis ($272,715 − $255,778 = $16,937).

However, there are other advantages to paying off the mortgage besides the numbers because there are risks to the 100 percent RRSP strategy that don't exist when you choose to pay down the mortgage instead.

Advantages to Paying Down the Mortgage

Here are the reasons I would consider paying down the mortgage instead of maxing out your RRSP contributions (even if the numbers supported the RRSP option). We reviewed three of these reasons in Chapter 3, but I think it is important to emphasize them again here, plus I have added to the list.

Guaranteed Rate of Return

The mortgage has a set rate of interest, and you will save exactly that rate on an after-tax basis when you pay down the related debt. The rate on your RRSP is unknown. You may make 4 percent after fees, as we have projected, but you may not. What happens if you are overexposed to the stock market and the market crashes again and you end up making much less than 4 percent, or possibly even losing money? Paying down the mortgage would have been a much better strategy.

Forces You to Be Fiscally Prudent

Barring an unforeseen gift like a lottery win or an inheritance, you simply can't pay down debt if you spend more than you make. Trying to pay down debt forces you to watch your spending and encourages you to increase your income because you can't make progress otherwise.

If you choose the RRSP route and don't actively attack paying down debt, it is easy to fool yourself into thinking you are on the right track. Many people who make RRSP contributions borrow the funds to do it because they are spending more than they make each year. They are therefore only able to make the contributions because their other debt (e.g., credit cards or lines of credit) is rising. Taking your eye off the pay-down-debt ball increases the likelihood that you'll never pay it down.

Provides Free Income Protection Insurance

If you own your house and are 100 percent mortgage-free and you can no longer work due to illness or an accident, you are much less likely to lose your house because you no longer have to make those monthly mortgage payments. That is why I recommend you try to become mortgage-free as soon as possible, and hopefully before retirement.

It's Easy to Measure

It is very easy to see where you are on your quest to get debt-free: it's the principal balance of the debt that is still owing. With the RRSP option, even with tools like the Procrastinator's Number Cruncher, it's difficult to know if your RRSP is large enough to fund your retirement, as there are so many variables that you can't control, such as inflation, investment return rates, tax rates, and how long you are going to live.

Optimizing RRSP Values

There is another issue we need to address. In our three options, Mike's RRSP is a lot larger than Nancy's. This is not ideal because it means the majority of the taxable RRSP withdrawals will be reported on Mike's tax return during the years of retirement.

A better option is to balance out the RRSP values so that withdrawals can be split evenly between spouses, which results in optimal splitting of the income during retirement and lower taxes. One very effective way of doing this is by the use of a spousal RRSP.

Spousal RRSPs

In a spousal RRSP, the contributor (in this case, Mike) makes the contribution based on his allowable limits; he gets the deduction at his marginal tax rate, but it goes into his spouse's or common-law partner's RRSP, so the spouse or common-law partner is the owner or annuitant. The benefit is that withdrawn amounts are taxed in the annuitant's hands. If he or she is in a lower tax bracket, there could be significant tax savings.

However, there is one important proviso: if funds are withdrawn within three taxation years of any contribution to the plan, the withdrawal will be reportable by the contributor spouse or partner, effectively undoing the strategy.

I changed the answer to the questions about spousal RRSPs on the "Questions" tab to say that Mike would like to make spousal RRSP contributions, but how do we know what percentage to allocate to spousal RRSPs? It gets back to our objective of balancing out the RRSP values as best we can.

Have a look at the RRSP values under the 100 percent RRSP option at the end of Year 10. It shows Mike's value as $503,800 and Nancy's at $81,445 for a total of $585,245.

It would be better to have each at a value of half that amount, i.e., $292,622.

I used Excel's "Goal Seek" function to determine the best percentage to allocate for Mike.

EXCEL'S "GOAL SEEK" FUNCTION

This is one of the most useful Excel functions there is. You simply select "Tools" from the main menu and then "Goal Seek."

All you do is point to the cell you are trying to optimize so it shows up in the "Set cell" box, then type the value you want to make that cell into the "To value" box. Then go to the "By changing cell" box and point to the cell you want Excel to change to reach your desired result.

Mike Uses a Spousal RRSP

In this case, using the "Goal Seek" function, I entered Nancy's RRSP value cell at retirement on the Summary Results tab to a value of $292,622, asked to change the cell that has the percentage that Mike wants to make to spousal RRSPs, and asked it to solve. The answer was 154 percent, which obviously can't be done since you can't allocate more than the amount available. The next best answer was 100 percent to get Nancy's RRSP up to the highest amount possible, so I changed the answer on the "Questions" tab to allocate 100 percent of Mike's RRSP contributions to a spousal RRSP.

Warning: During the last three years before their retirement, no spousal RRSP contributions can be made because the withdrawals would have to go on Mike's return, not Nancy's.

As the Clarks will be withdrawing from Nancy's spousal RRSP to fund their retirement starting in the year Mike turns sixty-six, I manually reduced the spousal RRSP allocation to zero during the last three years of Mike's pre-retirement contributions.

The results are the following RRSP values at retirement, which total $585,245:

- Mike $363,228
- Nancy $222,017

So the Clarks' net worth at the end of the year Mike turns sixty-five will be as follows:

Option 2: 100% RRSP	
	End of Year 10
Assets	
House	$487,598
RRSP — Mike	$363,228
RRSP — Nancy	$222,017
Total Assets	$1,072,843
Liabilities	
Mortgage	$179,322
Total liabilities	$179,322
Net Worth	$893,521

Note: The total net worth is the same as when Mike was not making spousal RRSP contributions, but the amounts in each RRSP are different.

Pension Income Splitting

Even though the Clarks are using the spousal RRSP option, it will still be worth it to use pension income splitting because their RRSPs are not of the same value. That is why I answered "Yes" to the question for Mike: "Would you like to split your pension income with your spouse?"

This will result in optimal splitting of Mike's mandatory registered retirement income fund (RRIF) withdrawals after he turns seventy-one and has converted his RRSP to an RRIF. If not, Nancy would be reporting only her CPP, OAS, and a smaller amount from her RRIF.

In Chapter 6, we'll start with these retirement figures to determine if the Clarks have enough saved for retirement and to find the best ways to access their various funds during their retirement.

CHAPTER FIVE

Your Pre-Retirement Investment Strategy

•

IN ORDER TO BUILD YOUR RRSP portfolio to its maximum size before your retirement, it will be necessary for you to spend some time and effort. Even if you have an advisor whom you trust, you'll need to be vigilant to make sure you understand what is happening in your account. As in any segment of the population, there are good and bad advisors. The problem is that many people use advisors who are simply salespeople, selling investment products that are profitable to them and their firms but very expensive for the people who buy them. These costly products are not going to help you meet your goals.

Do You Have a Good Advisor?

The following is a list of positive attributes of a good advisor and their firm.

They Listen as Much as They Talk

If you ask your advisor a question, how do they respond? A good advisor will always listen to your question, ask questions of you to clarify your situation, and give you a succinct answer in plain language.

A poor advisor is easy to identify. They babble on endlessly, using jargon you don't understand, and they are good at emotional selling. If your advisor wants to talk about general things (e.g., how the kids are, the weather, the local sports team) and doesn't like to talk about fees or how well your investments are performing, start the hunt for someone else immediately.

They Are Qualified

The term "financial advisor" is not well regulated in any province other than Quebec. It is relatively simple for someone to take a course allowing them to sell mutual funds and then call themselves a financial advisor.

However, a good advisor will have a professional designation (e.g., Certified Financial Planner, or CFP), which requires them to pass proficiency exams and be subject to supervision and regulation.

In Canada, anyone trading securities or who is in the business of advising clients on securities must be registered with the provincial or territorial securities regulator (unless an exemption applies). The regulators register only firms and individuals that meet certain standards.

The problem with securities regulation is Canada is that we don't have a formal national securities regulator; each province or territory has its own. To deal with this issue, the Canadian Securities Administrators (CSA) was formed. It is an umbrella organization of Canada's provincial and territorial securities regulators whose objective is to improve, coordinate, and harmonize regulation of the Canadian capital markets. See www.securities-administrators.ca to confirm the registration of your advisor or potential advisor. The category of registration tells you what products and services an individual or firm can offer. Note that CSA provides the following warning: "Being registered, however, doesn't mean that all firms and individuals have the same skills, provide the same services or charge the same fees. Make sure you understand their qualifications, and the products or services they are selling you."

Useful Statements

The good news is that investment firms now have to give you an annual statement showing all the fees you were charged, including any hidden fees like mutual fund trailer fees (a commission that the salesperson of a mutual fund receives each year that an investor remains in the fund), as well as commissions on any bond trades. They also have to give you your money-weighted personal rate of return after fees, which is the most important figure when it comes to monitoring your investments because it incorporates contributions and withdrawals to your account.

Unfortunately, they only have to disclose this information once a year, usually in December. So have a look at last December's statement and do a rough calculation. Take the total fees and divide by the average portfolio market value for the year. This will give you your average cost in percentage terms. Then look at your average rate of return. It's best to use the return they have generated for you for a longer period of time than the most recent year because the current year may not be typical. So use the return since you started with your advisor. Say your annual costs are 1 percent and they have been making you 5 percent on average per year. Well, no problem, you are in good hands. But if they are charging you, say, 3 percent per year and you are making 3 percent per year, they are taking 50 percent of your gains. That's not reasonable, and you should seek someone else to handle your money.

Registration Categories

The following are the main categories of financial services firms and advisors.

Firms
Investment Dealer
A firm that sells a broad range of investments including shares, bonds, exchange traded funds (ETFs), mutual funds, limited partnerships, real estate investment trusts, and exempt products such as shares in a private company. Some offer advice and a full range of services such as market

analysis, securities research, and portfolio management. Others act more like brokers, buying and selling securities based on your instructions. Investment Dealers must be a member of and follow the rules of the Investment Industry Regulatory Organization of Canada (IIROC). IIROC approves what products and customer types the Investment Dealer and its representatives can deal in.

Mutual Fund Dealer

A firm that sells only mutual funds. Except in Quebec, Mutual Fund Dealers must be a member and follow the rules of the Mutual Fund Dealers Association of Canada (MFDA).

Scholarship Plan Dealer

A firm that pools your contributions in a registered education savings plan to invest in scholarship plan units.

Exempt Market Dealer

A firm that sells exempt products. Exempt products can be sold without a prospectus. A prospectus is a legal document that gives investors important information about the investment (such as risk, fees, suitability, etc.). Without this disclosure, exempt products offer less protection to investors.

Restricted Dealer

A special kind of registration used for firms that do not quite fit under any other category. Securities regulators will tailor each restricted dealer registration with specific requirements or conditions.

Portfolio Manager

A firm that provides advice, manages your investment portfolio, and buys and sells on your behalf according to the instructions or discretionary authority you have given.

Restricted Portfolio Manager

A firm that provides advice about a particular sector or industry (such as real estate, oil and gas, biotech, etc.). Securities regulators will assign restrictions tailored to the firm's expertise.

Investment Fund Manager

A firm that manages an investment fund.

Individuals
Dealing Representative

A person who buys or sells investment products on your behalf based on your instructions. What they can buy or sell depends on the registration category of the firm that employs them.

Advising Representative

A person who provides advice on investment products. They can manage your investment portfolio according to your instructions. They can also make decisions and trades on your behalf. Advising Representatives are employed by Portfolio Managers.

Associate Advising Representative

A person who provides advice under the supervision of an Advising Representative.

Ultimate Designated Person

The chief executive officer of a registered firm. They are responsible for their firm's overall compliance with securities law.

Chief Compliance Officer

A person who manages a registered firm's day-to-day compliance with securities law.

Advisor Enforcement

Consult www.securities-administrators.ca to check your current advisor's status. If you are unhappy with your advisor, you should switch, but check the status of the other advisor first.

It is also possible to find out if there have been any disciplinary proceedings, charges, or convictions against registered advisors. Go to www.securities-administrators.ca, click on the "Enforcement" section, and then click on "Disciplined Persons."

Ensure you do this before you hand over any money to a new advisor!

Advisor Services

When it comes to personal finances, you will probably need more than one person to take care of your needs. You'll need a lawyer to help with your will, an accountant to do your taxes, a banker to handle credit, and a financial advisor to handle the rest of your financial needs, such as saving for your children's education and investing for your retirement.

The problem is that while it is relatively straightforward to hire a lawyer or an accountant, finding the right financial advisor is not. That's because there is a lot of confusion about exactly what their role is.

There are two main services that your financial advisor(s) will provide: financial planning and investment advice and administration. These are two very distinct roles.

Financial Planning
This involves a comprehensive analysis of all your financial issues, taking into account your financial situation and goals. It involves many areas such as investing, tax, estate planning, debt analysis, and more, and it often results in a written financial plan about how to achieve your financial goals.

Investment Advice and Administration
This involves the actual buying, selling, and rebalancing of your portfolio of investments.

Deciding on Roles

In some cases, one individual or firm performs both functions, while in others there are two separate firms involved. Many people assume that one person or firm is all they need, but this may not work for you because advisors are usually paid a commission for the sale of products to their clients.

If your advisor is being paid a commission on the sale of products, it makes it very difficult for them to provide independent professional advice (the more expensive the product you buy, the bigger the commission!). There is no real incentive for them to spend time analyzing your whole financial situation because they are not getting extra money to do that, and it may also result in them recommending a product or strategy that would reduce their income. For example, if an advisor makes a commission based on selling you RRSP investments, are they likely to recommend that you stop making RRSP contributions and pay down the mortgage? It's unlikely. And an aggressive commissioned salesperson may even encourage you to borrow to buy more!

It's important that you do your due diligence before hiring any type of advisor.

Your Advisor Options

Mutual Fund Dealer

I once had a client who had just emerged from bankruptcy, and her advisor was strongly pushing her to take out a loan to make an RRSP contribution. She couldn't control her spending but was being advised to immediately load up on more debt! It didn't make sense, but this kind of sales advice is often the result when there is a financial incentive to sell, sell, sell.

Mutual fund dealers are one type of advisor frequently used by Canadians. If you have this type of advisor, you are limiting the investments they can buy on your behalf. There is no doubt that there are some mutual fund dealers who give their clients good advice, but many do not, and the main reason for that is fees!

If you own mutual funds, you should be aware of the "Fund Facts" document. It is a summary of key information about your mutual funds, including visible fees such as deferred sales charges (DSCs), the management costs of the fund (often referred to as the management expense ratio, or MER), and rate of return information.

For many equity funds in Canada, the MER is more than 2 percent. That means that mutual fund managers have to beat the comparative benchmark index (a standard against which the performance of a mutual fund can be measured, e.g., the S&P TSX Composite Index) by that amount to leave you with what you could have made if you'd simply bought an investment that mirrored the index.

In other words, you are paying for active management to do better than passive management. With passive management, the people running the fund simply buy the stocks or other investments that make up the benchmark index. This is usually a much cheaper option than mutual funds because these investments, called exchange-traded funds, do not have to pay sophisticated professionals to research and pick the investments.

Generally, the only way your mutual fund dealer gets paid is by commission, which includes both visible and invisible fees such as trailer fees. These fees are tied to the product and essentially lead to a conflict of interest.

Which fund do you think your advisor would rather sell you: Fund A, which pays him and his firm a trailer fee of 0.75 percent a year, or Fund B, which pays them 0.15 percent a year? Of course, it is Fund A. Which fund would be better for you? Fund B.

It's a total conflict of interest.

Investment Dealer/Portfolio Manager

Investment dealers and portfolio managers aren't limited to just mutual funds. They can purchase stocks, bonds, ETFs, and a broad range of other products on your behalf. It makes sense to consider using this type of advisor. Why limit yourself to mutual funds?

These advisors can charge commissions just like mutual fund dealers, but there is another option that is more common: a percentage of assets under administration. For example, you pay a percentage of the average value of your investment account in a year, perhaps 1 or 2 percent. This separates the advice from the product so that your advisor has no incentive to sell you costly products and can include low-cost options like ETFs in your portfolio.

Discount Broker

If you are willing to do all the research, trading, and rebalancing of your portfolio yourself, using a discount brokerage account will cut your fees to the lowest possible amount. You'll just pay commissions to buy and sell the securities. There are many discount brokers to choose from, including ones from the big banks. You need to be careful, however, as it is easy to get too involved, make too many trades, and erode your returns with excessive commission fees.

Robo-Advisor

Most robo-advisors are start-ups by people with experience in the investing industry. They use computer algorithms to build portfolios based on a client's risk tolerance, goals, and personal profile. They automatically rebalance periodically so the target mix of stocks and bonds is maintained. Some robo-advisors offer light financial planning, but the main attraction is having your portfolio run for you at a low fee. Typical fees are 0.5 percent of the portfolio as opposed to 1 or 2 percent for human investment dealers.

Fee-Only Financial Planner

A fee-only financial planner offers comprehensive independent financial planning advice for a visible fee. The fee is usually an hourly rate or a fixed price.

These people may have one or more of these various designations:

- Chartered Professional Accountant (CPA)
- Certified Financial Planner (CFP)
- Chartered Life Underwriter (CLU)

- Personal Financial Planner (PFP)
- Registered Financial Planner (RFP)
- Trust and Estate Practitioner (TEP)

In most cases, they are not licensed to sell investments, so you'll have to either do that yourself or pay someone else to handle the buying, selling, and administration of your investments.

Fee-only planners charge average hourly rates from $100 to $500, and fees for a comprehensive financial plan are in the $2,000 to $3,500 range.

Fee-Only Financial Planner and Discount Broker

An option that is likely to become increasingly popular is to combine the services of a fee-only financial planner with a discount brokerage account to actually do the investing. The advantage of this arrangement is that not only do you get independent financial planning advice, you also minimize the costs of investment administration.

This is not for everyone, but if you are willing to spend some time and can resist the urge to trade too often, it could be a great way to bring down your investment costs. For example, if you pay a management fee of 1.5 percent a year to your advisor for financial advice and investment management and your portfolio has an average market value of $400,000, you'd pay $6,000 each year in fees. If you used a fee-only financial planner, you could pay $3,500 once for the comprehensive financial plan and then several hundred dollars for their time once or twice a year to review your progress and make recommendations about any changes. That would save you thousands of dollars a year in fees.

Advice from an Expert

Warren MacKenzie, CPA, CA, Head of Financial Planning at Optimize Wealth Management, is an expert in various aspects of retirement planning and investing. He recently wrote an article about how individual investors can take control and improve their investment results, and the following are his top ten tips.

Know the Difference between Investment Professionals and Salespeople

The exposure most people have to the financial services sector is through individuals who are licensed as salespeople. These people may or may not have any investing expertise, and, in many cases, they have a total conflict of interest. In other words, they have an incentive to sell you financial products that make money for them, and that money comes directly out of your pocket. In many cases, they are only licensed to sell mutual funds. They can't buy individual stocks, bonds, or exchange traded funds.

There are better alternatives.

For example, you could hire a full-service investment dealer licensed to sell a whole range of investment products, including stocks, bonds, and ETFs. These professionals usually have a designation, such as a Chartered Financial Analyst (CFA).

Don't Be Overconfident

If you think you can get ahead by trading individual stocks in your own account, think about who you are competing against. Most trading is done by professionals who probably have more information, discipline, experience, and tools than you. They are most likely the ones on the other side of each buy or sell you make. Do you honestly think that over time you are going to do better than they will?

You may also think it's possible to research a company so you know everything about it and are therefore able to predict its future stock price. The problem is that the stock market is very unpredictable. The prices of stocks are affected by many things, including global conflicts, unexpected innovations, new competitors, government intervention, social trends, and interest rates, to name a few. These items can come out of the blue and cause large swings in the value of any company. Just because you are smart and spend many hours researching investments doesn't mean you'll do well.

Working on your own is also dangerous because people tend to fall in love with their own ideas. This causes people to hang on to winners too long ("It's done so well for me, I can't bear to sell it now!") or delay in dumping losers ("It'll come back, I'll just wait a few more weeks"). Regardless of which option you choose, it makes sense to have another person to challenge your ideas.

Follow a Disciplined Investment Approach

If you don't have an investment process, you tend to be guided by your emotions. This is a recipe for disaster. If you don't have a "sell" strategy, you don't have an investment strategy. For example, you should have a simple and effective strategy to rebalance your portfolio according to guidelines laid out in a written investment policy statement.

Many do-it-yourself investors hold too many small investments. Even if some of these investments doubled in value, it wouldn't make a significant overall difference. They also tend to hold complicated securities that make it difficult to understand fees, asset mix, and inherent risk. Also, many hold legacy mutual funds where it is difficult to know what types of investment products are in them, therefore making it difficult to stick to an optimal asset mix (i.e., allocating your investments among different asset classes to help minimize risk and potentially increase gains, or "not putting all your eggs in one basket").

No one can consistently time the market. Don't fool yourself into thinking that you can get in and out of the market at the right time — even the professionals can't. That is why you need a written investment policy statement and some assistance from other people.

The key to getting ahead with investing is to reduce your trading activity. If you are constantly buying and selling, you are reducing your chances of success and increasing the drag that trading and other fees have on the performance of your investments.

Focus on Managing Risk

What overall rate of return on your portfolio are you aiming for? You can't answer that question without first determining what your goals are. If you can reach the amount you need to retire with a return of 4 percent, you should not have an asset mix designed to make 6 percent. This is especially important when you have ten years or less to build your retirement nest egg. That's because aiming for the higher rate will necessitate exposing more of your money to the volatility of the stock market.

Many people put themselves in a very risky situation when it comes to required rates of return. They don't take control of their spending and consequently don't have much money to invest. They therefore need a high rate of return to get to the required portfolio value. But hoping for a 10 percent rate of return to solve your problems will mean you'll have to take extreme risk. Chances are good this strategy will result in dismal failure because potential high returns come with the risk that they will be low or even negative. You can't afford that risk with ten years or less to go.

Managing risk also means you need to be diversified, by sector as well as by geography. If you want exposure to the stock market, you need to look beyond Canada, which has 70 percent of its market in just three sectors: financial, energy, and materials.

It's also important to understand your tolerance for risk. In a rising market, we all tend to think we have a high tolerance. It's only in a falling market that we can accurately gauge our tolerance level. Remember 2008–2009, when the S&P TSX Composite Index lost almost half its value in less than a year? If this kind of swing caused you to panic and sell, you found out the hard way that your tolerance for risk was lower than you thought.

Focus on the Big Picture

If you don't know what you are trying to achieve with your savings, you can't know the rate of return you'll need to get there.

But what if you are significantly short of your retirement goal and even a great investment return won't solve your problems? In this case, you'll really need to focus on the big picture, including cutting your spending and reducing debt.

It also makes sense to consider estate issues because, as we know, you can't take it with you. This means actively monitoring your investments throughout your retirement. A big mistake could mean having to reduce your lifestyle or explaining to the kids that their inheritance isn't what it used to be.

Avoid an Emotional Response

Money does not have a personality. It makes no difference whether you accumulated your money via a disciplined savings program, an inheritance, a bonus, or a lottery win. It should all be managed with the same level of care.

And don't expect the current trends to continue. You can't bet that interest rates will stay at the ultra-low rates of today for years to come; you don't know whether the current low oil prices are going to recover soon or whether it will take years. The same goes for the stock market. Will the U.S. market continue to defy gravity and reach new highs? If so, for how long?

As a general rule, investors should do the opposite of what their gut is telling them. They should sell in a market that has risen significantly and buy into a market that has dropped substantially. That is easier said than done and again stresses the importance of an investment policy statement with specific target asset allocations.

Measure Your Performance

Do you check how well your portfolio is performing? Most people don't bother looking at their statements annually to determine how well their advisor has been doing for them. You need to compare your personal investment rate of return to the fees you are paying so you can gauge your results.

These results also should be compared to a benchmark, which is usually measured by an ETF of the same composition as your portfolio. What good is paying an investment manager a fee to produce a return that is less than you could have received using ETFs in a discount brokerage account?

According to MacKenzie, many investors are underperforming the benchmark by 2 percent per annum. On a $250,000 portfolio, underperforming by 2 percent a year over ten years would cost you over $50,000.

Pay Attention to Income Tax

If you have money in a regular investment account in addition to your RRSP and TFSA, you need to be cognizant of income taxes. Your investment mix can make a huge difference to your after-tax rate of return. For example, equity investments beat interest income when it comes to taxes because capital gains on stock sales are only 50 percent taxed and dividends are taxed at a lower rate than interest.

But don't allow your portfolio to become overexposed to risky equities just because of the beneficial tax treatment. If you can't handle potential losses, then stick to a larger percentage of interest-paying fixed income investments regardless of the tax hit. And don't avoid selling a stock that has done well for you simply to avoid the capital gains tax. In other words, don't let the tax tail wag the investment dog.

Don't Act on Bad Information

Contrary to what many people think, some professional managers do consistently beat the market. Few mutual funds, however, beat their relevant benchmark index, largely due to fees, over-diversification, and plain bad luck.

Simple strategies like "buy and hold" may not work well either. In a rising market, the strategy works well, but not so in a bear market. For example, in 1989, the Japanese Nikkei Index had a high of just under 40,000 points; today it is just over 23,000. Over that period, you would not have wanted to be a Japanese buy-and-hold investor.

Be Logical in Your Analysis

Many people focus too much on fees. Fees are a necessary part of the equation, but they can only be judged when compared to the value received. Any fee is too much if no value is being received, but high fees may be justified if significant value is added. That value should be measured in a performance report that shows rate of return (net of fees) compared to the relevant benchmark index.

The services provided can also go beyond fees. Professional advice that prevented you from losing half your portfolio due to proper diversification is very valuable. The advice would have saved you a lot even though you had a negative return.

It's also important to distinguish between investment income and cash flow. Investment income consists of interest, dividends, and capital gains. When you retire, you'll need cash flow from your investments to pay the bills. Some investors overlook potential cash flow from the sale of stocks and mistakenly assume they need to be exclusively in securities that pay interest and dividends. In other words, you could sell some of your investments and eat into your capital to generate cash flow.

Investors often fool themselves into feeling better in a down market by telling themselves, "It's only a paper loss." If you bought a stock at $10 and it is now worth $2, make no mistake, you have lost money. Failing to recognize this fact simply delays taking advantage of the capital loss for tax purposes. Again, this is where independent advice can be important. You may not wish to admit you bought a loser, so you hang on in the hopes it will rebound. An outside expert can help you swallow your pride and take the hit before things get even worse.

Don't act on tips from your friends or colleagues. They are often based on faulty information and usually don't work. Even if the tip does work, it might have been obtained by insider information, in which case anyone acting on it may face legal consequences.

Don't put all your eggs in one basket. If you invest 100 percent of your money in equities, not only are you putting yourself at a higher risk than necessary, you'll have nothing to rebalance with (i.e., when markets go down, you'll want to be able to sell some fixed income securities to have the cash to buy stocks while they're cheap; if all your investments are in stocks already, you'll have no cash to buy more).

If you are unsatisfied with the investment management services you are getting, now is the time to find an independent professional who will satisfy you. Remember, the next ten years are going to be key to build your portfolio before your retirement. Don't accept the status quo; find someone who will help you realize your goals.

A Rule of Thumb that Makes Sense

I am not a big fan of rules of thumb because often they lead people astray, as there is rarely a single right answer to a personal financial issue. But when it comes to investing, one rule of thumb makes a lot of sense to me.

It says that the maximum percentage of equities in your retirement portfolio should be the result of one hundred minus your age, i.e., your age is the minimum percentage you should have in fixed income products. For example, a thirty-year-old should have a maximum of 70 percent in the stock market and a seventy-year-old should have a maximum of 30 percent in stocks.

This makes sense because it forces you to reduce your investment risk as you age, when you have less time to make up for any decline in the stock market.

Is the rule of thumb right in your situation or not? This subject is one that your financial planner should be addressing with you both now and later as your situation changes.

PART TWO

•

The Retirement Years

CHAPTER SIX

How Much Will You Spend During Retirement?

•

THE RULE OF THUMB SAYS you will need 70 percent of your pre-retirement income to maintain your standard of living after you retire. The assumption is that your expenses will decline by about 30 percent once you stop working.

In most cases, your expenses will decline. For example:

- You won't be paying CPP or EI premiums, and your income tax bill will also decline as your income does.
- You'll probably spend less on your car operating costs because you no longer travel to and from work each day.
- You'll eat lunch out less since you'll be home more often.
- You will pay less for dry cleaning as you won't be wearing business clothes.

But some costs may go up. For example, if you choose to travel more, your vacation costs will increase. (However, you may be able to mitigate vacation costs since your time is more flexible and you can travel in off-peak seasons that cost less.) Depending on your health, your medical and dental costs may increase. You may also have to pay to take care of your aging parents, or maybe even your children if they haven't been able to establish themselves financially.

So calculating the amount of money you'll need to set aside for retirement based on a rough rule of thumb can be misleading. True financial planning should be based on an analysis of existing expenses, not a percentage of income.

As we have seen with the Clarks, expenses can decline for reasons other than retirement. We saw a large annual reduction of $6,751 when they paid off their car loan. There was a huge yearly savings of about $18,000 after their daughter, Sophia, graduated from university, and when they paid off their mortgage, their annual cash outflow decreased by $21,753.

In most cases, significant expense reductions occur for reasons other than retirement, so when projecting expenses you must take into account the timing of these other events. To accurately plan for meeting your retirement expenses, you have to project future costs on a line-by-line basis and also consider the effect of inflation.

The Effect of Inflation

The general measure of inflation in Canada is the Consumer Price Index (CPI). The Bank of Canada currently has a mandate to keep inflation at approximately 2 percent a year, so it is often around that percentage. However, you cannot simply multiply your total expenses by overall inflation to project future outflows because inflation affects each line of your spending differently. For example, your mortgage costs are not affected by inflation, they are affected by interest rates. The same applies to your car loan or lease payments, but your car's operating costs are affected by inflation, and car insurance seems to increase every year. However, at the time of writing, the cost of gas had actually decreased, so that spending line has been subject to deflation.

The Clarks' Future Costs

Let's have a look at what the Clarks are likely to spend in retirement.

The following chart shows what they are projected to spend in Year 10, the last year of work for Mike at age sixty-five and Nancy at age sixty-three, assuming they opted to make RRSP contributions and therefore had not paid off the mortgage. (Note that I have ignored taxes because we don't yet know what their income is going to be after they retire.)

THE CLARKS' ANNUAL EXPENSES — YEAR 10		
	Expense	% of Total
Auto		
Auto fuel	$2,855	4%
Auto general	$426	1%
Auto insurance	$1,462	2%
Auto loan	$6,751	8%
Auto licence & registration	$220	0%
Auto repairs and maintenance	$416	1%
	$12,130	15%
Family		
Cash withdrawals	$5,000	6%
Clothing	$3,000	4%
Donations	$300	0%
Entertainment	$900	1%
Groceries	$5,000	6%
Insurance (life, income protection)	$3,213	4%
Meals out	$4,266	5%
Medical & dental	$1,219	2%
Miscellaneous	$1,219	2%
Vacation	$6,000	8%

THE CLARKS' ANNUAL EXPENSES — YEAR 10		
	Expense	% of Total
	$30,117	38%
House		
Mortgage	$21,753	27%
House Insurance	$1,462	2%
Utilities (heat, hydro)	$4,280	5%
Property tax	$4,266	5%
House repairs & maintenance	$3,535	4%
Security	$537	1%
Phone & Cable	$1,755	2%
	$37,588	47%
Interest and Bank Charges		
Bank Charges	$120	0%
Total Expenses	$79,955	100%

Let's think about the rule of thumb: what will change in their first year of retirement to make these expenses go down by 30 percent? There doesn't seem to be much opportunity to reduce their expenses: the mortgage won't be paid off, and the car loan still has another year to go. There may be some discretionary expenses they can reduce (like meals out and vacation), but there is not going to be any appreciable reduction in their spending just because they retire. That fact is the key to this book and to your plans for retirement.

Now for the good news! When the Clarks pay off their mortgage, their annual expenses will decline by $21,753 to $58,202, ignoring inflation. If the Clarks had chosen to pay off the mortgage instead of maxing out on RRSPs, they would already be in this position.

The other good news is their four-year car loan will be paid off in one more year, and they will no longer have the $6,751 in loan payments.

We'll discuss the issue of how best to finance your car in Chapter 16.

We'll make reasonable assumptions about the Clarks' spending over the next twenty years (the remainder of Mike's life), and we'll assume inflation averages 2 percent per year over that time.

Auto

We'll assume the Clarks will use the car less than when they were working. Let's say they will only drive two-thirds of the kilometres they used to, so we'll therefore reduce the fuel costs in Year 11 to $1,900 ($2,855 x 2/3). We'll assume the other operating costs rise by inflation. The Clarks will also buy a new car every eight years (as they have been doing), and we'll estimate they will receive $2,500 when they dispose of their old one. This is a conservative assumption because in retirement they'll probably be driving less so cars often last longer.

Family

We'll assume that the first five items (cash withdrawals, clothing, donations, entertainment, and groceries) go up by inflation each year. We'll assume they stop paying for life and income protection insurance. We'll keep meals out, miscellaneous, and vacations at the same amount. We'll assume medical and dental costs increase by 20 percent a year to $4,000 and then stay at that amount.

House

We'll assume that all the housing costs increase by inflation each year and that the mortgage will be paid off in ten years when Mike is seventy-five.

Interest and Bank Charges

We'll leave these at the same amount.

Total Retirement Expenses

The following is a summary of the Clarks' projected expenses for their retirement years until Mike is eighty-five years old.

THE CLARKS' ANNUAL EXPENSES — RETIREMENT						
Year	Age	Auto	Family	House	Interest and bank charges	Total
1	65	$12,130	$30,117	$37,588	$120	$79,955
2	66	$11,225	$27,432	$37,905	$120	$76,682
3	67	$4,563	$28,014	$38,228	$120	$70,925
4	68	$5,214	$28,660	$38,558	$120	$72,552
5	69	$5,799	$29,382	$38,894	$120	$74,195
6	70	$3,415	$30,194	$39,238	$120	$72,967
7	71	$11,623	$31,114	$39,588	$120	$82,445
8	72	$11,721	$31,794	$39,945	$120	$83,580
9	73	$11,821	$32,121	$40,308	$120	$84,370
10	74	$11,922	$32,453	$40,219	$120	$84,714
11	75	$5,274	$32,794	$40,598	$120	$78,786
12	76	$5,938	$33,140	$19,691	$120	$58,889
13	77	$6,536	$33,413	$20,084	$120	$60,153
14	78	$4,167	$33,766	$20,487	$120	$58,540
15	79	$12,391	$34,125	$20,897	$120	$67,533
16	80	$12,504	$34,492	$21,315	$120	$68,431
17	81	$12,618	$34,867	$21,740	$120	$69,345
18	82	$12,735	$35,248	$22,175	$120	$70,278
19	83	$6,103	$35,637	$22,618	$120	$64,478
20	84	$6,784	$36,035	$23,070	$120	$66,009
21	85	$7,399	$36,440	$23,532	$120	$67,491

The next step is to use the Number Cruncher spreadsheet (see Chapter 4) to see if the Clarks' income from their CPP, OAS, RRSPs, and RRIFs are going to be sufficient to pay for these estimated expenses.

The Findings

The year after Mike retires, at age sixty-six, his only source of income is his CPP and OAS, totaling $25,754. Nancy retired the same year at age sixty-three. The next year, when she is sixty-four, she has no CPP, as she has elected to start at age sixty-five, and no OAS, as she is under sixty-five.

But the Clarks' estimated expenses are $76,682, including $21,753 in mortgage payments, so they will have to withdraw from their retirement savings to cover the expenses. In fact, the Clarks have a shortfall for the first nine years of their retirement. So how do we figure out how much they have to withdraw from their savings to pay their expenses and how much each should withdraw? We'll use the Procrastinator's Number Cruncher spreadsheet.

Retirement Tax Tip

The rules say that we have to convert our RRSP into an RRIF by December 31 of the year we turn seventy-one. We then have to make required minimum withdrawals from our RRIF. (Note: Alternatively, you can buy an annuity, which we'll discuss in Chapter 10.) Annuity and RRIF payments are eligible for the pension income amount, which is a non-refundable tax credit of $2,000 federally and from $1,000 to $2,000 provincially or territorially. The problem is that regular RRSP withdrawals are not eligible for the pension income amount. So, if you need the funds, it makes sense to trigger an early transformation to an RRIF so the withdrawals are eligible for the pension income credit.

I have triggered an early conversion of Mike and Nancy's RRSPs to RRIFs at the ages of sixty-six and sixty-four respectively, and I have used Excel's "Goal Seek" function to calculate the required withdrawal amounts in excess of the mandatory RRIF withdrawals. Note that I have made Nancy's RRIF withdrawals equal to Mike's because "Goal Seek" can't solve for two independent variables.

Here are the results:

Mike's Age	Mike's Total RRIF Withdrawals	Nancy's Total RRIF Withdrawals	Combined Total RRIF Withdrawals
66	$27,422	$27,422	$54,844
67	$17,326	$17,326	$34,652
68	$18,072	$18,072	$36,144
69	$18,715	$18,715	$37,430
70	$17,495	$17,495	$34,990
71	$23,717	$23,717	$47,434
72	$24,107	$24,107	$48,214
73	$24,275	$24,275	$48,550
74	$24,438	$24,438	$48,876
75	$19,432	$19,432	$38,864
Total	**$214,999**	**$214,999**	**$429,998**

Will the Clarks have enough saved to finance their retirement to age eighty-five? The answer is yes, they will have more than enough.

The Number Cruncher shows that during the rest of Mike's life, the Clarks can cover their expenses with their CPP, OAS, and RRIF withdrawal amounts. The estimation shows they will even have excess cash during those years, which will be invested in their TFSAs.

When Mike dies at age eighty-five, Nancy will have plenty of income to live on for the last two years of her life. Here is the situation at the time of Mike's death:

Asset	Value
RRSPs	$303,485
TFSAs	$136,854
House	$724,545
Total Assets	**$1,164,884**

It seems the Clarks will have excess funds to cover their basic expenses for the rest of their lives. They can even afford to spend more and enjoy their retirement to the fullest and still leave a sizeable estate for their kids.

But you may not be in the same position as the Clarks, so the remainder of this book is dedicated to dealing with issues affecting your personal situation. We'll look into each situation so you can prepare for the best retirement possible.

CHAPTER SEVEN

Maximizing Your Canada Pension Plan

•

THE CANADA PENSION PLAN IS a mandatory government-sponsored pension plan that came into effect on January 1, 1966. Quebec is the only province that elected to create its own plan, the Quebec Pension Plan (QPP), which is similar to the CPP but is supported by the provincial government.

All Canadian employees, employers, and self-employed people have to contribute to the CPP. Contributions are required as soon as you reach the age of eighteen and are no longer required after you opt out at age sixty-five, or reach the age of seventy, or become disabled.

Monthly CPP pensions are paid to retirees, surviving spouses or common-law partners of deceased contributors, orphans, the disabled, and children of the disabled. The term "common-law partner" came into force on July 30, 2000, and replaced the former term, "spouse." A common-law partner is defined for CPP purposes as "a person who is cohabiting with the contributor in a conjugal relationship at the relevant time, having so cohabited with the contributor for a continuous period of at least one year." This means that same-sex couples are also eligible for CPP survivor's benefits.

A lump-sum death benefit of a maximum of $2,500 is also paid to the estate of deceased contributors. The amount is dependent on the contributions the deceased made to the CPP during his or her lifetime.

It is important to note that the monthly benefits paid under the plan are adjusted annually, based on increases in the Consumer Price Index, the most common measure of inflation in Canada.

In short, the CPP is an inflation-adjusted defined benefit pension plan that is paid until you die.

How Your CPP Premiums Are Calculated

Regular CPP premiums for employees in 2020 are calculated at a rate of 5.25 percent of earnings above an exemption of $3,500 to a maximum of $58,700. In other words, if you make under $3,500, you pay no CPP premiums, but if you earn between $3,501 and $58,700, the amount you pay is based on your earnings. If you earn $58,701 or more, you don't pay any more premiums above the maximum.

Here are the key figures for 2020:

Yearly maximum pensionable earnings	$ 58,700
Yearly basic exemption	$ 3,500
Yearly maximum contributory earnings	$ 55,200 ($58,700–$3,500)
Yearly maximum contributions	$ 2,898 ($55,200 x .0525)

How Your CPP Pension Is Calculated

The maximum monthly CPP retirement pension is equal to 25 percent of the average of the last five years' maximum pensionable earnings (YMPE). This is referred to as the average yearly maximum pensionable earnings (AYMPE).

Here's how they calculated the maximum monthly CPP retirement pension for 2020.

LAST FIVE YMPE	
2016	$54,900
2017	$55,300
2018	$55,900
2019	$57,400
2020	$58,700
2016 to 2020 AYMPE	$56,440
25% of the AYMPE	$14,110
Monthly pension ($14,110/12)	$1,175.83

How the CPP Is Adjusted for Inflation: The YMPE

The YMPE is increased each year by the ratio of the average industrial aggregate (average weekly earnings as determined by Statistics Canada) during the twelve-month period ending June 30 of the preceding year to the average industrial aggregate during the corresponding period one year earlier. From 2019 to 2020, the YMPE increased by 2.3 percent because the average weekly earnings increased by that same percentage.

CPP Pension Increases

After you begin to receive the CPP pension, the government uses the Consumer Price Index to adjust your CPP pension amount so that the benefits keep up with the cost of living.

The CPP pension is adjusted once a year using a twelve-month moving average method, which helps to smooth out fluctuations that may occur in a single month. The rate used to increase the CPP pension is the average monthly all-items CPI for the prior year's twelve-month period ending in October. They use October because they need to publish the rates for the next year in the fall.

Note that if the cost of living decreases over a twelve-month period, the CPP pension does not decrease but stays at the prior year's level. Also, while your CPP contribution rates increase every year by inflation, the retirement pension is calculated on the average of the last five years' YMPE, so it may lag behind current inflation.

The CPP Rules

Significant new rules regarding the CPP were approved in Bill C-51, which passed into law on December 15, 2009. These rules are as follows.

Penalty for Early Election

The normal age to elect for your CPP retirement pension to start is age sixty-five. You can elect to receive it as early as age sixty, but there is a cost if you do. The penalty for early election is a reduction of 0.6 percent for each month that you elect to start receiving your pension before you turn sixty-five, or 7.2 percent per year.

Premium for Deferring Election

You can also elect to delay receiving your CPP pension after age sixty-five up to as late as age seventy. In this case, you get a premium of 0.7 percent per month, or 8.4 percent per year.

Work Cessation Test Eliminated

Before 2012, for two months — the month before the CPP retirement pension was to begin and the month it did begin — you had to stop working or earn less than 25 percent of the CPP maximum pensionable earnings for the year of retirement and the preceding four years during those months. Now, those under sixty-five who elect to receive the CPP early do not have to undergo a work cessation test.

Post-Retirement Benefit (PRB)

Under the old rules, you could elect to start receiving your CPP before age sixty-five, then go back to work, and you would no longer have to pay CPP premiums on your earnings. Under the new rules, working beneficiaries under sixty-five are required to pay premiums to increase benefits. These premiums are the same as the regular premiums that everyone pays on their salary and self-employed earnings.

Like the CPP retirement pension, the amount of each PRB will depend on your level of earnings, the amount of CPP contributions you made during the previous year, and your age as of the effective date of the PRB.

For each year that you make a valid contribution to the CPP while receiving your retirement pension, you become eligible for a PRB the following January.

The maximum PRB for one year is equal to 1/40 of the maximum CPP retirement pension. If you contribute less than the maximum, the amount of the year's PRB will be proportional to your contributions. For example, if you contributed 50 percent of the maximum contribution level, you will receive 50 percent of the maximum PRB.

If you pay any amounts into your PRB one year, the amount of CPP pension you receive the next year, and every year thereafter, will increase (in addition to any inflationary increases).

After age sixty-five and up to age seventy, you can opt out of continuing to pay CPP premiums by filing form CPT30, "Election to Stop Contributing to the Canada Pension Plan, or Revocation of a Prior Election."

There is also an online calculator that gives you an estimate of the yearly benefits you could receive from the PRB for a single year of contributions, based on your employment earnings for the year and your age. To see the table that is relevant to you, choose your year of birth from the pull-down menu. The calculator is at www.canada.ca/en/services/benefits/publicpensions/cpp/retirement-income-calculator.html.

Increased Drop-out Provision

In calculating how much CPP you will receive, you are allowed to drop 17 percent of years of low earnings where you paid less than the maximum into your CPP. This means the number of years you can drop is eight, since there are forty-seven years from age eighteen to age sixty-five ($47 \times .17 = 8$). Note that it is irrelevant when these years were, whether early or later in life.

CPP Enhancements

The CPP is currently being gradually enhanced. This means you will receive higher benefits in exchange for making higher contributions. The CPP enhancement will only affect you if you work and make contributions to the CPP.

The enhancement increases the CPP retirement pension, post-retirement benefit, disability pension, and survivor's pension you may receive. Eligibility for CPP benefits is not affected.

Up until 2019, the CPP retirement pension replaced one-quarter of your average work earnings. This average is based on your work earnings up to the YMPE limit each year, as we just saw.

The enhancement means that the CPP will begin to grow to replace one-third of the average work earnings you receive after 2019. The maximum limit used to determine your average work earnings will also gradually increase by 14 percent by 2025.

Your CPP pension will increase based on how much and for how long you contribute to the enhanced CPP. The enhancements will increase the maximum CPP retirement pension by up to 50 percent for those who make enhanced contributions for forty years.

The enhancement also applies to the CPP post-retirement benefit. If you are receiving the CPP (or QPP) retirement pension and you continue to work and make CPP contributions in 2019 or later, your post-retirement benefits will be higher.

How Much Will Your CPP Retirement Pension Be?

The way the government calculates the amount you will receive from your personal CPP pension is complex. It is based on the amount you paid in from the month you turned eighteen to age sixty-five (or earlier if you elected early).

You cannot assume you will receive the maximum amount. In fact, most Canadians have not paid in enough to receive the maximum. According to the federal government, the average CPP retirement pension (at age sixty-five) in 2019 was $8,074.44, whereas the maximum was $14,110. That means most Canadians are receiving less than 60 percent of the maximum.

It is a good idea to consult a financial advisor who specializes in pensions. One advisor I consult when I need detailed information about the CPP (and OAS) is Doug Runchey of DR Pensions Consulting. He has over thirty years of experience working for the government on those two programs (see www.drpensions.ca). Doug has written a detailed article on how you can calculate exactly how much you will receive from your CPP retirement pension (see http://retirehappy.ca/how-to-calculate-your-cpp-retirement-pension).

If you find the process too confusing or complex, you can email DR Pensions at drpensions@shaw.ca along with your CPP Statement of Contributions and any questions you may have about your CPP retirement pension calculation, and he will help you for a small fee. (Disclaimer: I do not receive any compensation for referring people to DR Pensions; I do it because it is a very valuable service that is difficult to find.)

CPP: Should I Elect Early?

Unfortunately, just like most decisions related to personal finance, there is no easy answer. The main reason for this is that you need to know one important thing: How long will you live? That's a tough one to answer, but it makes a huge difference to your calculations.

For example, say you retire at age sixty and end up passing away at age sixty-eight. If you elected early, at age sixty, you would have received your CPP retirement pension at a reduced rate for eight years. If you had waited until age sixty-five, you would have received the full pension, but for only three years. If you make the calculations, you see that you would have been better off electing at age sixty because the greater number of years you collected the reduced pension outweighs the lesser number of years you collected the full one. The reduction penalty of 36 percent (five years at 7.2 percent per year) of the amount at age sixty-five is not overcome by waiting because you only get the higher amount for three years. However, if you live to the age of ninety-five, it would be best to wait until age sixty-five to receive your

CPP pension because you would be receiving the full amount for thirty years.

So what should you do? Since it is impossible to do a detailed calculation because we don't know how long we will be receiving the CPP pension, the best option is to go through a simple checklist that includes the important issue of taxes because the CPP pension is taxable when you receive it.

1. Do you need the money early?
   If the answer is yes, you need the money for groceries and other expenses, elect as soon as you can. End of story.
2. If you don't really need the money, are you in a low tax bracket?
   If you are in a lower tax bracket now and you may be in a higher tax bracket later, consider electing early if you could use the money.
3. Can you shelter your CPP pension from tax?
   If you have RRSP room, you could shelter it from tax by making an RRSP contribution for the same amount. If you are in a high bracket and have maxed out your RRSP room, defer electing until later since you will lose a significant portion to taxes depending on your tax bracket.
4. If the answer to the previous question was you have RRSP room to shelter your CPP, do you think the amount in your RRSP will grow at a higher rate than the penalty to elect early or the bonus to wait?
   Remember, the annual penalty for early election is 7.2 percent and the premium to wait is 8.4 percent. Those rates will be extremely difficult to beat after investment fees on a consistent basis.

To sum up, the government has achieved its objective of making early election less attractive to the majority of Canadians. It seems that waiting to receive your CPP pension is the best option unless you need the money or it is likely you will not live a long life.

Applying for Your CPP Retirement Pension

The simplest way is to sign in or register for a My Service Canada Account, located at www.canada.ca/en/employment-social-development/

corporate/online-services-forms.html. Alternatively, you can fill out and mail in form ISP1000, "Application for a Canada Pension Plan Retirement Pension."

TIP

When one spouse dies, it can have a significant effect on the total CPP pension amount that will be received by the surviving spouse. When a CPP contributor dies, CPP pays three kinds of survivor benefits:

- The death benefit: this is a one-time lump-sum payment (a maximum of $2,500 in 2020) paid to the spouse or the estate of the person who died.
- The survivor's benefit: this is a monthly benefit for the spouse or common-law partner.
- The children's benefit: this monthly amount is paid to a dependent natural or adopted child of the deceased contributor or to a child in the care and control of the deceased contributor at the time of death. The child must be either under age eighteen or between the ages of eighteen and twenty-five and in full-time attendance at a school or university.

To qualify for any or all of these benefits, the deceased contributor must have contributed to the CPP in the lesser of either one-third of the years in their contributory period (but no less than three years) or ten years. Your contributory period begins when you turn eighteen (or January 1, 1966, whichever is later) and ends when you start receiving your CPP retirement pension, turn seventy, or die (whichever happens earliest).

If you are receiving your CPP retirement pension and your spouse or common-law partner dies, you need to apply for a survivor's benefit. In this case, you will receive a combined monthly benefit.

CPP WARNINGS

- **Maximum benefit:** The amount of a combined survivor's/retirement benefit is limited to the maximum retirement pension. For example, if you begin receiving a combined benefit in 2020, the most you will receive is $1,175.83 a month. In other words, if you have been eligible to receive the maximum CPP pension because you contributed to the plan during your working life, you won't receive anything extra on the death of your spouse or common-law partner.
- **Survivor benefit:** If the surviving spouse or common-law partner is age sixty-five or older and not receiving any CPP benefits of their own, they are eligible for only a maximum of 60 percent of the contributor's retirement pension. It should be noted that the rules in this area are exceedingly complex for people under sixty-five, people with disabilities, and situations involving dependent children.
- **Old Age Security:** There's also the shock of the surviving spouse losing the deceased spouse's OAS pension — a maximum of $7,364.19 per year, in 2020. For couples on a tight budget, these issues can lead to significant financial difficulties for the surviving spouse or common-law partner.

CHAPTER EIGHT

Old Age Security: The Basics

•

THE OLD AGE SECURITY PENSION is a monthly pension provided by the federal government that is available to most people aged sixty-five and older who meet the Canadian legal status and residence requirements. You are entitled to receive the OAS pension regardless of whether you have worked or not.

If you are living in Canada, you must:

- be sixty-five years old or older,
- be a Canadian citizen or legal/permanent resident or landed immigrant at the time the government approves your OAS pension application, and
- have lived in Canada for at least ten years after turning eighteen.

If you are living outside Canada, the above rules are the same, except you must have resided in Canada for at least twenty years after turning eighteen.

If you have resided in Canada for at least forty years after turning eighteen, you should get the maximum. The OAS pension is adjusted for inflation every three months.

Currently, seniors have to apply to receive the OAS pension, and it is recommended that you apply at least six months before you are eligible to start receiving it. They are, however, phasing in an automatic enrollment process that will eliminate the need for many seniors to apply. The department that handles the CPP and OAS, Service Canada, will send you a notification letter the month after you turn sixty-four. If you don't receive this letter, you must apply for your OAS pension by applying online through your My Service Canada Account or completing and mailing in form ISP-3550, "Application for the Old Age Security Pension and the Guaranteed Income Supplement."

Your OAS Amount
In 2020, the maximum monthly amounts were as follows:

- January to March: $613.53
- April to June: $613.53
- July to September: $613.53
- October to December: $614.14

The total that a person could receive in 2020 was therefore $7,364.19.

OAS Clawback
The problem with OAS for higher income people is the clawback. In 2020, 15 percent of any net income before adjustments (line 23400 on your tax return) above $79,054 is clawed back from the OAS that was received. This is called the threshold amount.

Anyone with a net income of $128,149 or more would have had all their OAS pension clawed back. That is because 15 percent of the difference of $49,095 ($128,149 less $79,054) is equal to $7,364.19.

If you have to pay back a portion of your OAS, it will show as a deduction on line 23500 of your tax return as "social benefits repayment." This amount is deducted from line 23400 to give line 23600, your net income. The amount you owe is listed on the last page of your tax return on line 42200 as "social benefits repayment."

Old Age Security and Guaranteed Income Supplement

If you have low income, you may be eligible to also receive the Guaranteed Income Supplement (GIS), which provides a monthly non-taxable benefit to OAS recipients who have a low income and are living in Canada. You qualify for the GIS if you meet both the following criteria:

- You are receiving an OAS pension.
- Your annual income (or combined income if a couple), not including your OAS pension, is lower than the maximum annual income (currently $18,600 for singles and $24,576 for couples).

Voluntary Deferral

The government has brought in a rule that allows a voluntary deferral of the OAS pension for up to five years after the age of eligibility. If you elect to delay, you will receive a higher, actuarially adjusted pension when you do start to collect it. Your pension will be increased by 0.6 percent per month of deferral. That's 7.2 percent per year up to a maximum of 36 percent at age seventy.

This provision should be considered if you currently earn more than the threshold amount and expect future income to be under the threshold amount. In this case, you will get to keep more of your pension because it will be higher due to the monthly bonus.

Conclusion

When combined, your CPP and OAS pensions are unlikely to be sufficient to fund your retirement. However, they are guaranteed by the government, adjusted for inflation, and paid for your lifetime. That is a good, solid basis upon which to anchor your retirement.

CHAPTER NINE

Your Retirement Investment Strategy

•

WE HAVE ALREADY REVIEWED YOUR investment strategy leading up to retirement, so now we need to look at how that strategy may change after you retire.

Many people make the mistake of not altering their investment strategy when they retire, even though they should. Remember the rule of thumb that you should not hold a percentage of your investments in the stock market that is more than one hundred minus your age? That rule is even more important after you retire because significant stock market exposure during retirement puts you at extreme financial risk, and much of that risk is related to the timing of the stock market ups and downs.

Drawdown Risk

When you were younger and saving for retirement, the volatility of the stock market was not as significant because you had many years to regain any losses that you incurred. Look at the following chart showing two 100 percent stock portfolios.

Portfolio A shows how $200,000 would grow over a twenty-one-year period, assuming all the money was in an investment that mirrored the performance of the S&P/TSX Composite Index during the twenty-one years leading up to April 2020. Portfolio B uses the same rates but reverses the order of the stock market returns.

ACCUMULATION PHASE ON $200,000				
Age	Portfolio A Actual order		Portfolio B Reverse order	
45	7.4%	$214,800	-23.8%	$152,400
46	-12.6%	$187,735	22.9%	$187,300
47	-12.4%	$164,456	-8.9%	$170,630
48	26.7%	$208,366	8.1%	$184,451
49	14.5%	$238,579	22.2%	$225,399
50	24.1%	$296,076	8.4%	$206,466
51	17.3%	$347,298	10.9%	$228,970
52	9.8%	$381,333	12.7%	$258,050
53	-33.0%	$255,493	7.2%	$276,629
54	35.1%	$345,171	-8.7%	$252,562
55	17.6%	$405,921	17.6%	$297,013
56	-8.7%	$370,606	35.1%	$401,265
57	7.2%	$397,290	-33.0%	$268,848
58	12.7%	$447,745	9.8%	$295,195
59	10.9%	$496,550	17.3%	$346,263
60	8.4%	$454,839	24.1%	$429,713
61	22.2%	$555,814	14.5%	$492,021
62	8.1%	$600,835	26.7%	$623,391
63	-8.9%	$547,360	-12.4%	$546,090
64	22.9%	$672,706	-12.6%	$477,283
65	-23.8%	$512,062	7.4%	$512,602

ACCUMULATION PHASE ON $200,000		
Age	Portfolio A Actual order	Portfolio B Reverse order
Average rate of return	4.58%	4.58%

The interesting conclusion is that during the growth stage, the timing of the year-to-year rates is not that significant. The end result is the same: an average annual rate of return of 4.58 percent.

During the retirement phase, when you are drawing down from your retirement nest egg, however, the year-to-year timing can have a significant impact.

Here are two portfolios that are 100 percent invested in equities. The starting value is $500,000 in each case, and annual withdrawals are being made starting at $25,000 and increasing by 3 percent per year.

RETIREMENT PHASE ON $500.000						
Age	Portfolio A Actual order			Portfolio B Actual order		
	Return	Withdrawal	Account Value	Return	Withdrawal	Account Value
66	7.4%	$25,000	$510,150	-23.8%	$25,000	$361,950
67	-12.6%	$25,750	$423,366	22.9%	$25,750	$413,190
68	-12.4%	$26,523	$347,635	-8.9%	$26,523	$325,254
69	26.7%	$27,318	$405,841	8.1%	$27,318	$351,256
70	14.5%	$28,138	$432,470	22.2%	$28,138	$394,850
71	24.1%	$28,982	$500,729	-8.4%	$28,982	$335,135
72	17.3%	$29,851	$552,339	10.9%	$29,851	$338,560
73	9.8%	$30,747	$572,709	12.7%	$30,747	$346,905
74	-33.0%	$31,669	$362,496	7.2%	$31,669	$337,933
75	35.1%	$32,619	$445,664	-8.7%	$32,619	$278,751

Age	Portfolio A Actual order			Portfolio B Actual order		
RETIREMENT PHASE ON $500.000						
76	17.6%	$33,598	$484,590	17.6%	$33,598	$288,300
77	-8.7%	$34,606	$410,835	35.1%	$34,606	$342,741
78	7.2%	$35,644	$402,205	-33.0%	$35,644	$205,755
79	12.7%	$36,713	$411,909	9.8%	$36,713	$185,608
80	10.9%	$37,815	$414,871	17.3%	$37,815	$173,362
81	-8.4%	$38,949	$344,344	24.1%	$38,949	$166,806
82	22.2%	$40,118	$371,765	14.5%	$40,118	$145,058
83	8.1%	$41,321	$357,209	26.7%	$41,321	$131,434
84	-8.9%	$42,561	$286,645	-12.4%	$42,561	$77,853
85	22.9%	$43,838	$298,410	-12.6%	$43,838	$29,730
86	-23.8%	$45,153	$192,982	7.4%	$29,730	$0
Total Withdrawals	$716,912			$701,489		
Difference in Withdrawals	$15,423					
Difference in End Value	$192,982					
Total Difference	$208,405					

Portfolio A is lucky and has a good return in the first year of retirement. Portfolio B, on the other hand, has a very bad first year. Look at the value of the portfolios at the end of the first year of retirement, age sixty-six. Portfolio A has a value of $510,150 and Portfolio B has a value of only $361,950, which is $148,200 lower.

At age eighty-six, Portfolio B has been fully depleted with total withdrawals of $701,489. Portfolio A has provided total withdrawals of $716,912 and still has $192,982 left in it. Portfolio A is therefore

$208,405 ahead of Portfolio B due to the timing of the stock market returns.

This clearly illustrates the problem with being overexposed to the stock market. If you get really lucky, you might get the timing just right. But you could get very unlucky with the timing of stock market returns and end up significantly cutting your nest egg with no way to make up for it.

Now, this is an extreme example in order to illustrate a point. Few people would assume the risk of putting 100 percent of their retirement savings in the stock market at retirement age. If you are sixty-five when you retire, the rule of thumb we talked about would allow only 35 percent of the portfolio to be allocated to the stock market. This would reduce the chance of a major cut to your savings by limiting the amount at risk.

But what should you do with the rest of the portfolio, the portion allocated to fixed income? Guaranteed Investment Certificates (GICs) are worth considering.

Maybe Simple GICs Are All You Need

GICs are my favourite investment because they are easy to understand and you will always get your original money back. The two arguments I often hear against GICs are taxes and inflation.

The Tax Argument

The tax argument makes sense when we are talking about GICs in a regular investment account. That is because the interest you earn on a GIC is taxed as regular income at whatever marginal tax rate you are in. For example, if your GIC earns 2 percent in a year and you have to pay tax at a rate of 40 percent, your after-tax return would be a paltry 1.2 percent.

That is why I am a big fan of GICs, but only when held in tax-sheltered vehicles like RRSPs, RRIFs, and TFSAs. When held inside these types of investments, the interest accumulates either on a tax-deferred basis (in the RRSP and RRIF) or a tax-free basis (in the TFSA). So when we are talking about investing in GICs in our RRSP, RRIF, or TFSA, the tax argument does not exist.

One caveat: if you are very risk averse and can't afford losses in your portfolio, stick to GICs even if they are in a taxable account.

The Inflation Argument

The other argument is about the effect of inflation: Why would I invest in a GIC earning 2 percent a year when inflation is 2 percent and therefore my "real" rate of return is 0 percent?

The problem is the argument then goes on to suggest that you'd fare better in the stock market with higher returns to beat inflation. However, what if higher returns don't happen? What if you get unlucky with the stock market and lose almost 50 percent of your investment, as many indexes did in 2008/2009? How does that help you beat inflation? This type of thought process is often used to drive people's investment strategy and convince them to take a significant amount of risk — often more than they should.

There is no doubt inflation is a problem for retirees. Rising prices means the same money buys less in the future. So what is the best way to fight inflation? I would argue that fixed income products like GICs are actually quite good at fighting inflation: there is a correlation between interest rates and inflation because the central banks try to control inflation by adjusting interest rates. The Bank of Canada has an objective to maintain inflation, as measured by the Consumer Price Index, at about 2 percent. If inflation increases and prices rise at a greater rate, the bank will increase its key interest rate (the overnight rate). This sends a signal to the commercial banks to raise their prime lending and other rates. The rising cost of using debt tends to discourage consumers from borrowing, which means they spend less, and that leads to a slowdown in rising prices (disinflation).

The following chart shows the annual five-year GIC rate according to the Bank of Canada versus inflation as measured by the all-items CPI going back to 1958.

GIC RATES VERSUS INFLATION			
Year	GIC Annual 5-Year Rate	Inflation by All-items CPI	Difference GIC Over (Under)
1958	4.66	2.70	1.96
1959	5.28	0.70	4.58
1960	5.27	1.30	3.97
1961	4.96	1.30	3.66
1962	5.19	1.30	3.89
1963	5.15	1.30	3.85
1964	5.26	1.90	3.36
1965	5.52	2.40	3.12
1966	6.06	4.20	1.86
1967	6.34	3.40	2.94
1968	7.01	3.90	3.11
1969	8.03	4.80	3.23
1970	8.52	3.00	5.52
1971	7.75	3.00	4.75
1972	7.61	4.80	2.81
1973	8.19	7.80	0.39
1974	9.68	11.00	-1.32
1975	9.57	10.70	-1.13
1976	10.11	7.20	2.91
1977	8.96	8.00	0.96
1978	9.25	8.90	0.35
1979	10.40	9.30	1.10
1980	12.31	10.00	2.31
1981	15.36	12.50	2.86
1982	14.57	10.90	3.67
1983	11.52	5.80	5.72
1984	11.97	4.30	7.67
1985	10.80	4.00	6.80
1986	9.73	4.10	5.63
1987	9.61	4.40	5.21
1988	10.06	3.90	6.16
1989	10.31	5.10	5.21
1990	11.14	4.80	6.34
1991	9.30	5.60	3.70

GIC RATES VERSUS INFLATION			
Year	GIC Annual 5-Year Rate	Inflation by All-items CPI	Difference GIC Over (Under)
1992	7.75	1.40	6.35
1993	6.47	1.90	4.57
1994	7.27	0.10	7.17
1995	7.14	2.20	4.94
1996	5.72	1.50	4.22
1997	4.74	1.70	3.04
1998	4.47	1.00	3.47
1999	4.81	1.80	3.01
2000	5.34	2.70	2.64
2001	4.05	2.50	1.55
2002	3.91	2.20	1.71
2003	3.13	2.80	0.33
2004	2.92	1.80	1.12
2005	2.71	2.20	0.51
2006	3.16	2.00	1.16
2007	3.31	2.20	1.11
2008	3.01	2.30	0.71
2009	1.94	0.30	1.64
2010	1.97	1.80	0.17
2011	1.87	2.90	-1.03
2012	1.65	1.50	0.15
2013	1.63	0.90	0.73
2014	1.92	2.00	-0.08
2015	1.47	1.10	0.37
2016	1.42	1.40	0.02
2017	1.39	1.60	-0.21
2018	1.69	1.70	-0.01
2019	2.08	2.20	-0.12
Average	6.36	3.68	2.68

As you can see, GICs have historically done a good job of beating inflation: the annual GIC rate has been (on average) 2.68 percent higher over the sixty-two-year period.

Inflation has been higher in only seven years during that period: in 1974, 1975, 2011, 2014, and 2017 to 2019. Therein lies the problem — GIC rates of today are historically low, so they aren't beating inflation. But there is no solution to this problem. The answer is not to jump into the stock market: to do so would be incredibly risky and could backfire in a big way.

Many people wish that GIC rates would go back to the double-digit days of the 1980s, but the problem is a relative one. We need to remember that inflation was also in the double digits then — our investments did very well, but the rising cost of living devoured a lot of the gains.

We can't do anything to alter inflation, so that means we have to watch our spending, manage our cash flow, and minimize our taxes.

CHAPTER TEN

Registered Retirement Income Fund versus Annuity

•

BY DECEMBER 31 OF THE year you turn seventy-one, you must convert your RRSP to a registered retirement income fund or an annuity.

Converting Your RRSP before Age Seventy-One

What most people aren't aware of is that you don't have to wait until age seventy-one to convert your RRSP. You can choose to convert it to an RRIF or an annuity before that. From a tax point of view, this may make sense at age sixty-five because only annuity payments from an RRSP or RRIF payments are eligible for pension income splitting and the $2,000 pension income non-refundable tax credit (remember, that is what I did with the Clarks).

TIP

If you have a younger spouse, don't forget that the minimum withdrawal can be based on your age or your spouse's or common-law partner's age. It makes sense to choose whoever is younger since that will minimize your required withdrawals. But beware, you need to elect to do so prior to receiving any payments from the fund, so make the decision before you start! This option is only an advantage if you don't need the money to finance your spending. In other words, if you need more than the minimum required based on your age, basing it on your younger spouse is of no benefit.

RRIF or Annuity?

First, we'll discuss the most popular method: the RRIF.

RRIFs

Converting an RRSP to an RRIF is basically just changing the name on the account from RRSP to RRIF. Your RRIF contains the same investments that were in your RRSP when you converted it. However, once you convert your RRSP, you will have to start the minimum withdrawals. The withdrawal rate (the "prescribed factor") is set by the federal government and is applied to the market value of your RRIF on January 1 of each year to determine how much you must withdraw by December 31.

For those under age seventy-one, the withdrawal percentage follows this formula: Opening market value of the RRIF on January 1 × 1/(90 – age).

For example, in the year in which you were sixty-five on January 1 and turned sixty-six during the year, the percentage would be 1/(90 – 65), which is 1/25, or 4 percent. If your RRIF had an opening value of $400,000, the required withdrawal would be $16,000 ($400,000 × .04). Note that there is no maximum with an RRIF: you can take out more, or even all of it, but you will have to pay tax on the withdrawals.

The 2015 federal budget reduced the minimum withdrawal factors for ages seventy-one and older. Prior to the change, RRIFs that were set up before 1993 had lower minimum withdrawal factors than those set up after 1992. Starting in 2015, all plans use the new rates.

Here are the withdrawal rates effective since 2015:

RRIF MINIMUM WITHDRAWAL RATES FROM 2015	
Age (on Jan 1)	%
71	5.28%
72	5.40%
73	5.53%
74	5.67%
75	5.82%
76	5.98%
77	6.17%
78	6.36%
79	6.58%
80	6.82%
81	7.08%
82	7.38%
83	7.71%
84	8.08%
85	8.51%
86	8.99%
87	9.55%
88	10.21%
89	10.99%
90	11.92%
91	13.06%
92	14.49%
93	16.34%
94	18.79%
95 or older	20.00%

RRIF ADVANTAGES

- The main advantage of an RRIF over an annuity is that if there is anything left at the date of death of the last surviving spouse, the after-tax amount can be passed on through an inheritance. Your investments may do so well that your next of kin may be very happy!

...

> ### RRIF DISADVANTAGES
>
> - Apart from the government legislating how much taxable income you must take out of your RRIF each year, the main problem is that you could run out of money before you die. Maybe you made some bad investment decisions, paid fees that were too high, or simply took out more than you should have — or maybe it was a combination of these things.
>
> - When you die, the balance of your RRIF can pass tax-free to your surviving spouse or common-law partner. But when your partner dies, the market value of the RRIF at their date of death will be taxed on their final income tax return at their marginal tax rate at that time. If the RRIF has a high balance at their death, the tax bill could be significant.

Annuities

An annuity is a contract sold by an insurance company. You transfer money to them in exchange for their promise to pay you a certain amount of money for life. I am indebted to Kurt Rosentreter, CPA, CA (www.kurtismycfo.com), for the information on annuities in this chapter.

Factors Affecting Annuity Payments

The amount of each annuity payment is based on the following factors:

- The amount of money invested.
- Your age.
- Your gender.
- Interest rates in the market.
- The type of annuity.
- Features attached to the annuity (guarantee periods, number of lives, inflation indexing, etc.).

- Income deferral (time until payments start).
- Whether the payment is from a registered account (RRSP) or a non-registered account.

Each payment to a female is lower than one to a male because females generally live longer than males, so the insurance companies know they will probably be making more payments to a sixty-five-year-old woman than to a sixty-five-year-old man.

The older you are, the fewer payments you will receive over your remaining life, so the payments will be higher if you start at a later age.

Types of Annuities
Single and Joint Life Annuities
A single life annuity is based on one person's life. They are useful for single people or for the last surviving spouse.

A joint (or last to die) annuity is for couples seeking to guarantee an income stream until the death of the second spouse.

Guarantee Periods
What if you hand over $100,000 to buy an annuity and then die the next day? This is why there are guarantee periods. You can guarantee payments for five, ten, fifteen, twenty, or thirty years, but the longer the guarantee period, the lower the monthly payments.

Term Certain Annuity
This type of annuity guarantees payments for a pre-selected period of time, instead of for life. They are useful for covering fixed-period obligations such as the remaining amortization period of a mortgage.

Fixed versus Indexing
A fixed annuity maintains the payment throughout the term of the annuity. With an indexed annuity, the monthly payments are adjusted by an annuity factor to account for future inflation.

ANNUITY ADVANTAGES

- The main advantage of an annuity is that you can't run out of money because they are usually paid for life. With people living a lot longer than they used to, guaranteed cash for life is a significant benefit.

- Annuities are also low maintenance. Once you hand over the cheque, you just sit back and wait for the cash to come in each month. You don't have to worry about how your investments are doing.

ANNUITY DISADVANTAGES

- Since most annuities end with your death, there is nothing left to pass on to your beneficiaries through an inheritance.

- Due to the current low rates being offered by the insurance companies, many people feel they can do better with their own investments inside an RRIF.

- You will have much less flexibility than with an RRIF, which enables you to take out a lump sum to finance something such as a vacation or a new car.

How Much Will You Get?

It will depend on several variables, but here's an example.

The following chart shows the monthly annuity payment you would receive based on a premium of $100,000 paid from an RRSP with a ten-year guarantee period, beginning at different ages.

INSURANCE COMPANIES	AGE 65			AGE 70		
	Male	Female	Joint	Male	Female	Joint
BMO Insurance	$490.87	$449.04	$402.78	$563.91	$516.88	$460.80
Canada Life	$464.09	$427.04	$388.53	$534.82	$484.65	$439.59
Empire Life	$453.46	$416.97	$453.46	$519.43	$477.69	$519.43
Great-West Life	$464.09	$427.04	$388.53	$534.82	$484.65	$439.59

INSURANCE COMPANIES	AGE 65			AGE 70		
	Male	Female	Joint	Male	Female	Joint
La Capitale	$470.33	$418.45	$374.66	$543.41	$483.99	$431.34
RBC Insurance	$490.40	$448.19	$403.23	$564.43	$516.79	$463.07
Sun Life	$460.17	$422.16	$379.94	$538.61	$496.00	$437.94
Source: Lifeannuities.com, February 5, 2020						

These results show if you are a male, retired at age sixty-five, and you paid $100,000 out of your RRSP, the most you would receive from one of these companies is $490.87 a month, or $5,890.44 per year for life (from BMO Insurance). For a female, the top rate is only $449.04, or $5,388.48 per year, from the same company. And you can see joint rates are even lower.

If you started at age seventy, the maximum rates increase to $563.91 per month for males and $516.88 per month for females (again from BMO Insurance).

Let's look at the rates of return these payments would provide (in other words, the annual rate of return your RRIF would need to earn to be able to make the same payments as if you had left the money in your RRIF).

If you were male and lived until age eighty-five, the rate of return on your $100,000 annuity for that series of 240 payments of $490.87 would be 1.7 percent per year. If you lived until age ninety, the rate of return would be 3.3 percent, and if you lived until age ninety-five, the rate of return would be 4.23 percent per year. For a female, those returns for the monthly payments of $449.04 to age eighty-five are only 0.8 percent, 2.5 percent to age ninety, and 3.5 percent to age ninety-five. Do you think those are good returns based on how long you think you will live? If so, annuities may be worth a look.

However, as we have discussed, there are other advantages to annuities that make a decision based solely on rates short-sighted. The main advantage is the guaranteed payments, no matter how long you live. And that is worth a lot, as many people today are living longer than previous generations.

A Combined Strategy

There is no rule saying you have to choose to purchase either an RRIF or an annuity with 100 percent of your RRSP when you turn seventy-one. You could buy an annuity with some of your RRSP and leave the remainder in an RRIF.

This strategy makes some sense. First, to determine how much of an annuity to buy, you calculate what your core annual expenses will be, i.e., the expenses you know you are going to have to pay for the rest of your life. You then calculate how much of that amount will be covered by your other guaranteed income for life (your CPP, OAS, and any other defined benefit pensions) and buy an annuity to make up the difference. In this way, you have guaranteed you'll always be able to pay your core expenses, and you'll also have some funds inside your RRIF that may yield a better rate of return than the rates your annuity is paying. This may mean you will still have some money remaining so you can leave your kids an inheritance. Happy kids!

Tax Planning Opportunity

As we have discussed, the first $2,000 of eligible pension income qualifies for a federal non-refundable tax credit on your annual income tax return. Lifetime annuity payments from your RRSP as well as RRIF payments do qualify as eligible pension income; however, withdrawals from your RRSP don't.

So you could convert all your money to an early RRIF or buy an annuity. But there is an alternative that isn't so drastic. Assuming you need the money from age sixty-five to seventy-one (before you are forced to convert your RRSP to an RRIF or annuity), it would probably make sense to convert some of your RRSP to an annuity to pay out at least $2,000 per year. Alternatively, you could convert $14,000 of your RRSP to an RRIF and take out $2,000 each year from age sixty-five to seventy-one. In both cases, you'd be eligible for the pension income amount.

Note that the provinces and territories also have pension income tax credits ranging from $1,000 to $2,000. The federal non-refundable tax credit rate is 15 percent, and the provinces and territories range from 4 percent to 10.5 percent, so the $2,000 credit is worth between $351 and $449 per year in reduced taxes.

If your spouse does not have enough pension income to maximize their claim, it may make sense to take advantage of pension income splitting. In this case, increase the amounts above to $4,000 per year and transfer $2,000 per year to your spouse.

TIP

One of the best websites I have seen that explains Canadian tax and financial information is www.taxtips.ca. If you are seeking explanations about how taxes work in Canada, this is a good site to visit (please note I have no relationship with this website).

CHAPTER ELEVEN

Your Retirement Age

•

DELAYING RETIREMENT FOR EVEN ONE year can have a very positive impact because it's one more year that your earnings cover your expenses and one more year of RRSP contributions and growth of those funds. It's also one less year that your RRSP has to cover your spending. So it makes sense to give a lot of thought to when you are going to retire.

The flip side of this positive news is that you may not have a choice. Increasingly, companies are looking for ways to cut costs — and experienced employees in their late fifties and early sixties are easy targets.

But let's start with the good news. We'll look at the Clarks' situation using the Procrastinator's Number Cruncher (see Chapter 4) to see what the financial impact would be if they delayed their retirement for one year.

I have changed the answer to the question "At what age do you plan to retire and stop making RRSP contributions?" to sixty-six for Mike and sixty-four for Nancy. This means that Mike and Nancy continue to earn their salaries until the end of the year in which they turn sixty-six and sixty-four, respectively.

The chart below compares the end value of the Clarks' net worth assuming they retire in the year Mike turns sixty-five and Nancy turns sixty-three versus waiting for one more year. We need to compare the values at the same point in time — the end of the year in which they turn sixty-six and sixty-four.

If they retire at ages sixty-five and sixty-three, their RRSPs will continue to grow, but they also have to withdraw some money to fund their first year of retirement (the year in which they turn sixty-six and sixty-four). If they delay retirement to ages sixty-six and sixty-four, it is assumed that they would put 100 percent of any excess income into Mike's RRSP rather than pay down the mortgage.

	Mike Retires at Age 65	Mike Retires at Age 65	Mike Retires at Age 66
	Value at End of Year 65	Value at End of Year 66	Value at End of Year 66
Assets			
House	$487,598	$497,350	$497,350
RRSP — Mike	$363,228	$349,238	$423,968
RRSP — Nancy	$222,017	$205,590	$212,752
TFSA — Mike	N/A	N/A	$27,905
Total assets	$1,072,843	$1,052,178	$1,161,975
Liabilities			
Mortgage	$179,322	$164,413	$164,413
Total liabilities	$179,322	$164,413	$164,413
Net Worth	$893,521	$887,765	$997,562

Comparing the last two columns, we see that the Clarks' total net worth is $997,562 if they retire when Mike is sixty-six versus $887,765 if they had retired one year earlier. That's higher by $109,797.

Here is a summary of what makes up the difference:

- Mike's RRSP is higher by $74,730.
- Nancy's RRSP is higher by $7,162.

- Mike's TFSA is higher by $27,905 (because he maxed out his RRSP).

Think about how you much better you'd feel about financing your retirement years if you had that much more saved.

How to Make It Happen

In my book *Cash Cows, Pigs and Jackpots: The Simplest Personal Finance Strategy Ever*, I make the point that when it comes to cash inflows, you are the best cash cow you'll ever have. In other words, your ability to earn income is the biggest source of cash you're likely to have, and therefore it makes sense to nurture yourself. I make the case that proper diet, exercise, and sleep is the best way to make sure you keep on earning.

And of course, the better shape you are in, the lower your medical costs are likely to be as you get older. If you keep yourself in shape, not only will you feel better but you'll also be much more likely to be able to work past age sixty-five.

So what are you waiting for? Resolve to get in better shape immediately!

The Consulting Option

One of the advantages of being self-employed is that you have to develop the ability to find work. You can't survive if you don't because, unlike a job, you don't get a paycheque for showing up every day and working.

But those who are not self-employed and depend on a job their whole lives are at a distinct disadvantage if they get laid off before they had planned. That could result in serious damage to their retirement savings, as there are fewer years to build and more years of retirement to finance. If this is your situation, I encourage you to think about how to find clients who could use your skills in consulting or another role. In the later stages of our lives, we have a lot of experience that is of value to someone, but you need to figure out how to find them.

I have always found that developing personal contacts is the most efficient way of building a network. Develop a system to track potential clients and referral sources and then keep in touch with them.

After this pandemic has passed, invite your contacts out for coffee or lunch once in a while, or maybe even for a few drinks in the evening. Don't rule anyone out — I have found some of my best referral sources are those whom you might consider competitors. For example, other personal finance trainers have put me in touch with organizations that have hired me to give my half-day and full-day live webinars and pre-recorded courses.

TIP

Remember to keep a separate copy of all your valuable contacts in your own contact manager, like the one that comes on your personal smart phone. If all you have is the contact management system of your employer and you get laid off, you will have lost them all.

Conclusion

You may not have a lot of control over when you retire if you are subject to your employer's whims, or perhaps because of health concerns, but do yourself a favour and give some thought to when your ideal retirement date would be.

Remember, if you can extend it by even one year, it could make a significant difference in the amount of money you'll have to spend in your retirement.

CHAPTER TWELVE

How Long
Will You Live?

•

TO PLAN YOUR RETIREMENT SPENDING accurately, it would really help to know how long you are going to live. That is a tough question to answer — but that doesn't mean you shouldn't give it some serious thought.

What the Statistics Say

Statistics Canada has published a chart that shows the life expectancy (at birth and at age sixty-five) for residents of the Canadian provinces and territories for the period from 2016 to 2018.

The chart on the next page shows the current reality. In Canada, males who reach the age of sixty-five are likely to live to age eighty-four (nineteen more years), and females who reach sixty-five can generally expect to live to age eighty-seven (twenty-two more years).

Of course, you need to factor in your health and your family history. You may not live as long as the average person, or you may live longer. However, statistically you are unlikely to live to be ninety-five or one hundred years old.

So how does this affect your planning? As a starting point, you should assume that you need to budget for approximately twenty years of retirement after age sixty-five.

LIFE EXPECTANCY						
	At Birth		At Age 65		Years Left at Age 65	
	Males	Females	Males	Females	Males	Females
Canada	79.9	84.1	84.4	87.1	19.4	22.1
Alberta	79.2	83.8	84.3	87.2	19.3	22.2
British Columbia	79.9	84.6	84.9	87.6	19.9	22.6
Manitoba	77.9	82.2	83.5	86.4	18.5	21.4
New Brunswick	78.6	82.8	83.3	86.2	18.3	21.2
Newfoundland and Labrador	77.9	81.9	82.9	85.4	17.9	20.4
Northwest Territories	75.2	78.7	81.6	82.9	16.6	17.9
Nova Scotia	78.3	82.7	83.1	85.9	18.1	20.9
Nunavut	69.8	73.1	80.5	79.4	15.5	14.4
Ontario	80.3	84.4	84.6	87.4	19.6	22.4
Prince Edward Island	79.8	83.7	83.5	87.0	18.5	22.0
Quebec	80.9	84.3	84.5	87.0	19.5	22.0
Saskatchewan	78.0	82.7	83.8	86.9	18.8	21.9
Yukon	76.2	81.7	83.0	85.6	18.0	20.6
Source: Statistics Canada, Demography Division						

"Resting Heartbeat" Theory

There is an online calculator that predicts how long you can expect to live based on your resting heartbeat. It can be found at www.csgnet work.com/avglifeexpfromhr.html. The theory is based on the average healthy human heart with no other factors involved. According to Dr. Robert Jarvic, inventor of the artificial heart, the potential average number of heartbeats in a lifetime by a healthy heart is "greater than 2 billion." The American Heart Association says the average potential is 2.6 billion, and other organizations estimate a range from 2 billion to

2.9 billion. (Of course, all the estimates are qualified guesses that can't be verified.)

According to the website, the average heart rate for adult humans is 70 to 75 beats per minute in relaxed mode. Each person has different levels of stress and other factors, so your rate may be outside the average range. (Note that the site strongly suggests that if you are concerned about heart risk factors you should contact your doctor to address your concerns.)

The website uses default variables of 72 beats per minute and 2.6 billion lifetime beats. This yields an anticipated lifespan of only 68.66 years. (When I input my resting heart rate of 53 beats per minute I get a potential life expectancy of 93 years.)

Try it and see your result. It may even encourage you to exercise more to reduce your heart rate so you'll live longer. But beware, that will mean you'll have to save more for retirement!

Don't Worry, Be Happy!

Believing we are going to live to a ripe old age (e.g., ninety-five or one hundred) could have a negative impact on our lives because if we think we will need more money, we tend to adapt our behaviour, such as:

- scrimping and saving before retirement to build up a massive RRSP,
- not taking great vacations because we "can't afford it",
- constantly worrying about running out of money during retirement, thus making it difficult to enjoy our lives, and
- starting to think about how much is left for our kids to inherit, causing us to spend even less.

A CAUTIONARY TALE

One of my readers was very concerned about the possibility of living a long life, so he delayed his dream of taking an African safari because he thought he couldn't afford it.   ...

A CAUTIONARY TALE cont.

He and his family scrimped and saved every penny they could for decades. This meant they didn't go on vacations when the kids were still at home, they rarely enjoyed meals out at a restaurant, and they stayed in their small house instead of moving to a more comfortable home. Finally, they retired, but the worries about running out of money did not stop. "Maybe we'd better not go just yet, let's wait a few years and see how this retirement thing goes," was the refrain in their first few years of retirement. Finally, they decided it was time to go, and they started to plan their dream safari vacation. Sadly, at this advanced age he was unable to get health insurance for the trip, so their dream vacation never happened.

Maintaining Balance in Your Life

I am the first to admit that I am cheap. If I were on my own, I would have zero debt, a smaller house, and I would have maxed out my RRSP and TFSA and probably had savings outside in regular investment accounts as well. But I am fortunate enough to be married to a person who keeps me balanced. She convinced me to go on European vacations while the kids were young, and she talked me into buying a thousand-dollar video camera when our first child was born (iPhones did not exist yet!). In both instances, we really couldn't afford it, but what is the current value of those experiences and videos? Priceless.

You need to have balance. If both you and your spouse (if you have one) like to spend money, you need to create a budget and cut back and save more. On the other hand, if you and your spouse like to save money and are worried about financing your old age to one hundred (or more), perhaps you can afford to relax a little and enjoy life a bit more, before it's too late.

TIP

Remember that you are unlikely to ever actually run out of money. There are several reasons for that. First of all, if you are eligible for CPP and OAS, those are both inflation-adjusted and paid for life. You also possibly own your own home, which you could use as a source of funds (more about that in Chapter 15). And if you do start to run low, most people would adjust their spending habits to make sure they didn't spend everything too soon.

CHAPTER THIRTEEN

Old Age Health Care Planning

•

MEDICARE, CANADA'S HEALTH CARE SYSTEM, provides universal coverage for medically necessary health care services on the basis of need rather than the ability to pay. It is a publicly funded system composed of an interlocking set of ten provincial and three territorial health insurance plans that cover required hospital and primary care physician services. All Canadian citizens and permanent residents are eligible for public health insurance, and when you have insurance you don't pay directly for most health care services.

Health Canada's mandate is to help Canadians maintain and improve their health. Among other roles, their responsibilities include setting and administering national principles for the health care system through the Canada Health Act. This federal legislation puts conditions in place by which the provinces and territories may receive funding for health care services. Under the Canada Health Act, primary care doctors, specialists, hospitals, and dental surgeons are all covered by provincial insurance policies.

THE PROCRASTINATOR'S GUIDE TO RETIREMENT

Provincial and Territorial Plans

New residents to a particular province or territory must apply for health coverage; upon approval, they will be issued a health card that provides coverage in that province or territory. Certain provinces (British Columbia and Ontario) require health care premiums for services, but under the Canada Health Act, health services cannot be denied due to financial inability to pay premiums.

Each province and territory has its own health insurance plan that provides free emergency services, even if you do not have a government health card. If you have an emergency, go to the nearest hospital. If you go to a walk-in clinic in a province or territory where you are not a resident, you may be charged a fee.

Here is a list of the websites for the provincial and territorial ministries of health that are responsible for administering health care:

Alberta	www.alberta.ca/health-wellness.aspx
British Columbia	www.gov.bc.ca/health
Manitoba	www.gov.mb.ca/health
New Brunswick	www2.gnb.ca/content/gnb/en/departments/health.html
Newfoundland and Labrador	www.health.gov.nl.ca/health
Northwest Territories	www.hss.gov.nt.ca
Nova Scotia	https://novascotia.ca/dhw/
Nunavut	www.gov.nu.ca/health
Ontario	www.health.gov.on.ca/en
Prince Edward Island	www.princeedwardisland.ca/en/topic/health-pei
Quebec	www.msss.gouv.qc.ca/en/
Saskatchewan	www.saskatchewan.ca
Yukon	www.hss.gov.yk.ca

Health Insurance

Government health insurance plans cover basic medical services. You have to pay for any services that are not covered, or you can pay for private insurance to cover them. The following are generally not covered by your provincial or territorial plan:

- Certain prescription medications.
- Dental care outside hospitals.
- Certain ambulance services.
- Prescription eyeglasses and contact lenses.
- Laser eye surgery.
- Cosmetic surgery.
- Travel insurance.
- Private or semi-private hospital accommodation.

If you are employed, you may get coverage from your employer. These plans usually cover the items listed above, and some plans may even continue coverage after you retire (to certain limits).

It's not possible to list the details of coverage for each province or territory, so I'll address the health care coverage in the most populous province, Ontario. Consult the website for your province/territory as listed previously for your specific health care coverage.

The Ontario Health Insurance Plan (OHIP)

OHIP covers a wide range of health services that are funded by the Ministry of Health and Long-Term Care. The following is a summary of insured services.

Doctors

OHIP covers all medically necessary doctors' visits and treatments, including any tests that are provided by or ordered by your doctor. OHIP does not cover services that are not medically necessary (e.g., cosmetic surgery). Physicians usually charge for any uninsured services.

Hospital Visits and Stays

If you need to go to the hospital, OHIP covers:

- Doctor and nursing services.
- Services to diagnose what's wrong (e.g., blood tests and X-rays).
- Medications for in-patients (once you are discharged, prescribed medications are not covered).
- Some medications for outpatients.
- Accommodation and meals if you have to stay (private and semi-private rooms not included).

Abortions

OHIP covers the cost of surgical abortions that take place in a hospital or clinic. It also covers Mifegymiso, a pill that induces an abortion in early pregnancy, if you have a prescription from a doctor.

Dental Surgery in Hospital

Some dental surgeries need to be performed in a hospital because they are complex and/or you have another medical condition that needs monitoring during the procedure. OHIP covers in-hospital dental surgeries such as:

- fracture repair,
- tumour removal,
- reconstructive surgeries, and
- medically necessary tooth removal (prior approval by OHIP required).

TIP

Note that several universities and colleges have dental clinics open to the public and that the fees are usually lower than private practitioners' fees.

Optometry

OHIP covers the cost of one major eye exam (for vision and general eye health) every twelve months, plus any minor assessments you need, but only if you are:

- nineteen years and younger, or
- sixty-five years and older.

If you are twenty to sixty-four years old and you have a specific medical condition affecting your eyes that requires regular monitoring, OHIP will cover a major eye exam for you once every twelve months and any follow-up appointments related to the condition for a number of specific conditions.

Other medically necessary care (e.g., cataract surgery) provided by a medical doctor is insured. Uninsured services include the cost of eyeglasses, contact lenses, and laser eye surgery.

Podiatry

OHIP covers between $7 and $16 of each visit to a registered podiatrist (foot health specialist) up to $135 per patient per year, plus $30 for X-rays. You will need to pay for the remainder of the cost of each visit. Surgeries performed by podiatrists are not covered by OHIP.

Ambulance Services

If you need an ambulance for a medical emergency, OHIP covers part or all of the costs depending on the circumstances. For example, you are responsible for an ambulance copayment charge of $45 if your trip is within Ontario and a physician deems your ambulance services to be medically necessary.

Ontario Drug Benefit Program

The Ontario Drug Benefit (ODB) program is the public drug funding system of Ontario. It covers 4,400 prescription drug products contained in the provincial formulary.

People sixty-five years old and older are eligible for the Ontario Drug Benefit program if they have a valid Ontario health card. You don't need to apply for coverage and should receive a letter of notification of ODB eligibility by mail approximately three months before you turn sixty-five. The letter will let you know that you will automatically join the ODB program on the first day of the month after your sixty-fifth birthday.

The ODB program runs from August 1 to July 31 each year. You pay a portion of prescription drug costs based on your yearly income after taxes and marital status.

Currently, if you are a single senior with an income after taxes of more than $19,300 a year or part of a couple with a combined income after taxes of $32,300 a year, you fall into the higher income copayment category. You will pay the first $100 of total prescription costs each program year. This is called the deductible and is paid down when you fill your prescriptions. After you have paid the total $100 deductible, you will then pay up to $6.11 for each prescription. This is the copayment towards the ODB dispensing fee for each prescription for a covered drug in the benefit year. If your income is below these amounts, you pay up to $2 for each prescription filled or refilled.

The drug must be prescribed by an authorized Ontario prescriber (e.g., a family doctor) and purchased from an Ontario pharmacy that is online with the Ministry of Health and Long-Term Care's computerized Health Network System or from an Ontario doctor who dispenses prescription drugs. When both generic and brand name drug products are available, the ODB pays the pharmacist for the lowest cost alternative.

The ODB does not cover prescription drugs purchased outside Ontario, drugs that are not listed on the official Ontario Drug Benefit Formulary/Comparative Drug Index, or drugs that are not approved by the Exceptional Access Program.

Community-Based Health Services

Community-based services are also referred to as home care, home health care, in-home care, or outreach services. They help seniors and people with physical disabilities to live independently and remain in their homes as long as possible. They provide visiting health services at home to people with a disability, illness, or limitation due to aging who would otherwise need to go to, or stay in, a hospital.

Local Health Integration Networks (LHINs) arrange all government-funded services for people living at home. LHINs are responsible for deciding who receives care, the level of care needed, and for how long. These services used to be provided through Community Care Access Centres (CCACs).

A case manager will recommend the most appropriate services for you, based on an assessment of your needs. Your case manager will tell you what services your LHIN can provide and what's available in your community. Government-funded services are delivered by health professionals and personal support workers who are under contract with your LHIN. Your case manager will need to visit your home to assess your health. If you qualify, your case manager will create a customized home care plan that meets your specific needs. If your needs change, your case manager can reassess your health and adjust your plan of care. If you qualify for government-funded care, your LHIN will coordinate your application and select the provider for you.

Services include nursing care, physiotherapy, occupational therapy, speech-language therapy, social work, and healthy eating advice as well as personal care services such as bathing, dressing, eating, toileting, and transportation to appointments. Homemaking services include house-cleaning, laundry, shopping, banking, planning and preparing menus, and caring for children. Palliative care is also addressed. You can receive in-home services if you are an Ontario resident with a valid Ontario health card, adequate treatment can be provided at home, and your needs cannot be met as a hospital outpatient.

To contact your local LHIN, go to www.healthcareathome.ca or call the Seniors' INFOline toll-free at 1-888-910-1999.

Housing Choices for Seniors

Most of us would like to stay in our own homes as we age. If staying in your home or apartment becomes too difficult for you, you may want

THE PROCRASTINATOR'S GUIDE TO RETIREMENT

to consider a move. Seniors who are able to live independently have a number of housing options to choose from, some of which may include health and support services if needed. Let's look at the main options.

Staying at Home

To do this effectively, there are a number of services available:

- Community support. These services help people to remain in their homes when they are unable to take care of all their own needs. Services are non-medical in nature and include meal preparation and delivery, transportation, security checks, and visits. Organizations that provide these services may be either for-profit or not-for-profit.
- Home care. This refers to a range of services from personal care to nursing care. Most home care is government funded in order to get seniors out of hospitals and rehabilitation beds. To access this support, you need to go though the provincial central access system (as we have just discussed for Ontario). There are also private paid services available.
- Caregiving. Making sure senior are healthy, safe, and well cared for is an important and difficult task. The caregiving role is challenging emotionally, physically, and financially as anyone who has taken on the role of caring for an aging parent can attest.

Retirement Homes

These are operated by private businesses that offer various combinations of accommodation, support services, and personal care. They are almost always for-profit with no funding or regulation of care or support services by the provincial government. You are responsible for the entire cost of both the accommodation and care services, unlike long-term care facilities, which are subsidized by the government.

However, retirement home accommodation rates are subject to rent controls. Retirement homes vary widely in terms of care and services provided, amenities offered, types of accommodations, staffing patterns, and physical structure (from converted houses to high-rise buildings).

Costs vary widely and are dependent on the type of accommodation and the services provided.

Independent Living

These provide independent living residences for retirees in a community of seniors. Residents are typically functionally independent and able to arrange for any care services they need. Independent living is not licensed or regulated. Residences may include houses, apartments, condominiums, or life lease buildings. They are sometimes referred to as retirement communities, retirement homes, or seniors' housing. Amenities can include twenty-four-hour security, social interaction with other seniors, and leisure and recreational activities. The ownership structure can range from simple ownership to condominium, land lease, or life lease options. A life lease is a form of housing tenure generally developed for seniors that is similar to a condominium and is typically operated by non-profit or charitable institutions. A tenant is granted the right to occupy a dwelling unit in return for an up-front payment and monthly maintenance fee payments.

If the daily chores, including housekeeping and meal preparation, are becoming too much, independent supportive living is an option that offers such service.

Assisted Living

This refers to the provision of services that allow residents to age in place in a retirement home with light to medium supports before having to move to a nursing home or long-term care facility. These programs provide on-site personal support services including bathing, dressing, grooming, oral hygiene, eating, and assistance with medications. They can also help with wayfinding for those with mild Alzheimer's disease or other dementia. Nursing services may also be provided, and costs may or may not be government subsidized.

Long-Term Care Facilities

A senior who is no longer able to live independently in his or her own home, who requires more support than that offered by a supportive living environment, or who is at risk at home may require placement in a long-term care facility. They are designed for people who need twenty-four-hour on-site nursing services and daily personal assistance. They are provincially regulated and funded and are often referred to by other names, including nursing homes, extended care homes, intermediate care homes, homes for the aged, old age homes, special care homes, residential care homes, and continuing care homes.

You can't access long-term care directly: you have to contact your health region because eligibility for placement is governed by provincial legislation and access is controlled by gatekeepers, which differ by province or territory.

It generally must be shown that the applicant's care requirements can best be met in a long-term care facility and that none of the publicly funded community-based services or other caregiving, support, or companionship arrangements available to the applicant are sufficient to meet their requirements.

The government usually pays for all nursing and personal care services in long-term care facilities; however, residents must pay for their accommodation costs. The maximum amount residents can be charged for accommodation is determined by the province and is set out in regulations. Residents may choose to pay for additional services such as cable TV, telephone, and hairdressing.

The Cost of Care

When I need detailed information about financial planning, investing, and insurance, I consult Kurt Rosentreter, CPA, CA, CFP, an investment advisor and insurance agent with Manulife Securities. His website is www.kurtismycfo.com, and there you will find a number of excellent newsletters he has written. One of them addresses the realities of old age health care in Canada, and he has generously allowed me to use some of its content.

The newsletter notes that the health care system is difficult to navigate and can be expensive, despite the fact that it is quite good for short-term illness and injury. For example, if a Canadian has a stroke, the medically required services are covered (such as a physician, hospital care, and essential short-term hospital accommodation), but most government support ends there. The majority of necessary medical equipment (e.g., wheelchairs, hearing aids, and oxygen supplies) is not covered, nor are home safety modifications to make the home more accessible (e.g., wheelchair ramps and safety bars).

Since the Canada Health Act covers only physician access and hospital accommodation, the provinces vary widely in what is provided to those who require long-term care accommodation, personal home care, and other forms of long-term care.

Staying at Home

The decision to stay at home and receive care can also be a costly option. The newsletter cites an example of a seventy-nine-year-old man with advancing Parkinson's disease who has opted to stay at home. This high-needs client requires a lot of care per week:

- Thirty-five hours of personal care ($25 per hour).
- Fourteen hours of meal preparation ($23.95 per hour).
- Three hours of skilled nursing care ($49.60 per hour).
- Two and a half hours of laundry and housecleaning ($23.50 per hour).
- Twenty-four hours of companionship/supervision when his son and daughter-in-law are unable to look after him ($23.50 per hour).

The cost of each of these services is high (prices given are provincial averages that were current at the time of writing), and the total costs add up very quickly — to $8,300 per month in this case. Even with the government subsidy covering the cost of twenty hours a week of personal care and one hour a week of nursing, the net amount that must be paid is $6,100 per month, or more than $72,000 per year for this one person. And that doesn't factor in the cost of home modifications like wheelchair ramps, bathroom support bars, stairlifts, walk-in bathtubs, and power wheelchairs.

Long-Term Care Facility

As we know, the government usually covers the cost of health care in a long-term care facility, including personal care, nursing, and medication. But it does not cover the cost of accommodation and other services such as cable TV and telephones. These costs can really add up.

Let's look at the costs in one province, Ontario. The cost depends on the type of room, as follows (as of July 1, 2019):

- Basic room (four people sharing one room): $1,891.31 per month.
- Semi-private room: $2,280.04 per month.
- Private room: $2,701.61 per month.
- Short stay: $40.24 per day.

See www.ontario.ca/page/find-long-term-care-home for the current cost of care.

The downside to the low-cost option is longer waiting times. Because of the demand for this type of accommodation and the shortage of long-term care facilities, it is not uncommon for people to wait for months or even years for a spot to open up. Because of the demand, many people end up having to accept the first bed that becomes available, even if it is hundreds of kilometres from their home, family, and friends.

Retirement Home

For many people, a retirement home is a viable option, but the government does not cover the cost, so it can get expensive. Depending on the type of living arrangement and the extra care needed, costs can range from $3,000 to $7,000 a month with an additional $1,000 or more if extra care is needed.

Single Accommodation or Double?

A couple sharing a room is usually less expensive than two seniors living in separate accommodations. However, in many cases, only one of the spouses needs long-term care. If the healthier spouse still lives in the couple's house or apartment, the combined living costs increase significantly.

Income Tax Credits and Deductions

The Government of Canada provides a number of tax breaks to help reduce the cost of aging.

Medical Expense Tax Credit

You can claim eligible medical expenses for you, your spouse or common-law partner, or your children who were under eighteen at the end of the tax year. You can also claim eligible medical expenses that you or your spouse or common-law partner paid for any of the following people who depended on you:

- Your or your common-law partner's children or grandchildren who were eighteen years or older at the end of the tax year.
- Your or your common-law partner's parents, grandparents, brothers, sisters, aunts, uncles, nieces, or nephews who were residents of Canada at any time of the year.

A wide variety of costs qualify, including prescription drugs, dental work, eye care, cancer treatment, medically required home renovations, and walking aids. This is a non-refundable tax credit where only expenses in excess of the lesser of $2,352 (for 2019) or 3 percent of your net income can be claimed for the federal tax credit.

Disability Tax Credit

This non-refundable tax credit provides a break for people who live with a long-term mental or physical impairment that makes it difficult for them to perform everyday activities. A medical doctor must confirm eligibility. The maximum disability amount for 2019 is $8,416.

Caregiver Amount Tax Credit

This non-refundable tax credit is available if you support a spouse, common-law partner, or dependant with a physical or mental impairment. The amount you can claim depends on your relationship to the person for whom you are claiming the credit, your circumstances, the person's net income, and whether other credits are being claimed for that person.

For your spouse or common-law partner, you may be entitled to claim an amount up to a maximum of $7,140 plus $2,230 in the calculation of line 30300 (the spouse or common-law partner amount).

For an eligible dependant eighteen years of age or older (who is a person for whom you are eligible to make a claim on line 30400, amount for an eligible dependant), you could claim up to a maximum of $7,140, and you may also be entitled to claim an amount of $2,230 in the calculation of line 30400.

For an eligible dependant under eighteen years of age at the end of the year (who is a person for whom you are eligible to make a claim on line 30400), you may be entitled to claim $2,230 in the calculation of line 30400 or on line 30500 (caregiver amount for infirm children under eighteen years of age).

For each of your or your spouse's or common-law partner's children under eighteen years of age at the end of the year, you may be entitled to claim an amount of $2,230 on line 30500.

For each dependant eighteen years of age or older who is not your spouse or common-law partner nor an eligible dependant for whom an amount is claimed on line 30300 or line 30400, you may be entitled to claim an amount up to a maximum of $7,140 on line 30450 (caregiver amount for other infirm dependants age eighteen or older).

Also note that your province or territory will have its own tax credits and possibly grants related to aging. It is important that you hire a professional tax preparer with experience in this area to make sure you are minimizing your tax bill.

PART THREE

•

Special Situations

CHAPTER FOURTEEN

Attacking Debt

•

IN THIS BOOK, WE HAVE dealt with a fictitious family, the Clarks. We have travelled with them on a journey from being in credit card debt with ten years to go before retirement to having significant savings in their RRSPs to finance their retirement years. However, many Canadians do not have as many assets and have much more debt than the Clarks. For them, the journey is going to be tougher. Perhaps this applies to you? If so, this chapter will help.

Why Are People in Debt?

Before we get into the details of how to get out of debt, let's start with the root of the problem.

Anyone who has a balance of consumer debt they can't pay off, like credit cards, must at some time have been spending more than their income. In other words, their expenses and other cash outflows have consistently exceeded their take-home pay, which is their income after taxes and other withholdings like CPP and EI. The cash outflows might have been for vital things like groceries, mortgage payments, or education costs for their kids, or they could have been for discretionary items such as vacations or other items (e.g., a big flat screen TV, designer shoes, etc.) that are beyond the family's budget.

Many people extol the virtues of making the distinction between "wants" and "needs." This makes sense but is not always helpful because if you listed all the cash outflows in your life over the last year, you'd probably find that the majority of them fit into the "wants" category rather than the "needs" category. What are your basic needs? You need food, water, and shelter. But you don't need to eat out at fancy restaurants several times each week, you don't need a million-dollar house, and you don't need expensive vacations. Many people could survive on a much lower percentage of their income if they downsized their house and limited their spending to essential food and other basics.

That is why it is important to track your personal finances to see where your money is being spent because the only way to pay off your debt is to reduce your spending or increase your income (or both).

Tracking Your Spending

In our busy world, there are many excuses for not tracking our spending. Most people say they don't have time to do it because they've got too many other things to do, including their jobs and taking care of their families.

But what if there were a way to do it automatically with just a little effort from you? Then www.mint.com may be for you.

Mint.com

This website is a free site operated by Intuit, Inc., the makers of QuickBooks bookkeeping software.

Once you sign up and enter your personal banking information, the site automatically downloads your transactions, gathers all your personal financial information in one place, and presents the results to you in charts, graphs, and line-by-line details.

You are required to enter your banking and credit card usernames and passwords, so you need to satisfy yourself that your data is secure. There is a section on the website dealing with security that states they use measures like multi-factor authentication and Norton security to help ensure safe sensitive data transfer. However, you need to feel comfortable since you are giving them access to download your banking information.

They will send you a weekly email summarizing your spending as well as how you are doing with any budget categories that you have set up. You can even set up bill payment reminders, so you'll get an email to remind you to pay a bill. You will also receive suggestions and advice about ways to save money that are often accompanied by offers from financial institutions that have business relationships with Intuit. (That's one of the reasons the site is free!)

One of the most useful sections is the "Trends" section, where you can instantly see a chart of where your money has gone during the previous seven or fourteen days, month, or year. Here is an example of what that looks like by category:

Your Spending

CATEGORY	SPENDING
Home	$23,336.63
Food & Dining	$19,135.05
Travel	$12,712.01
Auto & Transport	$10,566.80
Misc Expenses	$6,527.05
Shopping	$6,008.97
Fees & Charges	$4,853.99
Health & Fitness	$3,747.79
Show more	$3,921.29
Total	**$90,809.58**
	Export to CSV

In addition to your spending, you can also get information on your income, net income, assets, debts, and net worth.

It is important to note the risks of disclosing online banking and credit card information to anyone, including third-party financial applications and online services. By disclosing online banking user IDs and passwords to a third party, you may breach your financial institutions' user agreements and be held liable for any losses resulting from unauthorized transactions despite any security measures the third-party service may have in place. Make sure to check with your financial institution before activating any third-party services requiring personal banking information.

Where Did All My Cash Go?

The most important step is to review where your cash has gone. What are the big money drains? Are there any expenses that are going to end in the near future? Are you surprised by how much you spent in certain areas? Did you spend a lot of cash? After this analysis, you should be fully aware of the problem areas in your spending.

Why Paying Off Debt Is Hard

If someone is overloaded with debt, it is usually because they have been living beyond their means. To get out of debt, it will be necessary to cut your spending to break even. If you reduce your spending to match your income, you will get to the point where you aren't adding new debt each month. But in order to pay off your debt, you have to be spending less than you make, which means you will have to cut even more of your spending and/or increase your income. In many cases, this will be very challenging because your spending cuts may have to be severe. However, it's what you'll have to do if you really want to gain control and pay off all your debt.

Credit Card Debt

The real problem with credit card debt is the high interest rate, especially for department store cards, which can be as high as 29 percent. To make matters worse, credit card interest often compounds on a monthly basis, so you are charged interest on interest. This is the opposite of what happens when you invest and compounding is working for you. In this case, compounding is working against you.

Here's a simple example. Say you had a $10,000 credit card balance owing at the beginning of the year at a rate of 20 percent interest per year. How much interest would you owe after the first year, assuming you made no payments during that year? You would expect it to be $2,000 ($10,000 x 20 percent), but the interest is actually $2,194 because the credit card company is calculating interest on interest every month.

In this case, the balance owing at the end of the year would therefore be $12,194, and that's assuming you didn't charge another dime to it for the whole year. Obviously, this makes getting out of debt much more difficult.

If you have revolving credit card debt at a high rate of interest, there are several options.

Option 1: Cancel Your Points Card/Department Store Card

Call your credit card issuer, cancel your high-interest points card, and replace it with a basic card. In many cases you can cut your interest rate in half very quickly, as the basic cards charge much lower rates. (We'll discuss the best points cards in Chapter 19 because they are only beneficial if you don't carry a balance.)

Option 2: Balance Transfer

The next option is to shop around for a better rate. Look for a balance transfer offer from another credit card company. These offers are constantly changing. I have seen offers ranging from zero interest for a year to 3 percent for six months on transfers. You can easily find and apply for cards that will accept a balance transfer online. Just Google "best credit card balance transfer offers" and you should find a number of sites to help. One of the best I have found is www.ratehub.ca. If you have a pretty good credit rating, it will usually be quite easy to get approved.

TIP

The top search result is often a sponsored one. That means the credit card company has paid to come first. Often that rate is not the best one. Remember to sort by rate and ignore sponsored ads. When I last checked, there were twenty different cards listed, including the following offers:

- MBNA True Line® MasterCard® credit card: 0.00% for ten months
- Scotiabank Value® Visa card: 0.99% for six months
- Tangerine Money-Back Credit Card: 1.95% for six months

Companies make these offers because they know the people involved are unlikely to change their habits and be able to pay off the balance at the end of the discount period. They then begin collecting the high interest. The key is to make sure you have a plan for when the introductory period expires. The best idea is to pay off the balance beforehand. The next best option is to make another transfer to a different low-rate card.

The Dangers of Debt Consolidation

One of the most common strategies for people in credit card and other high-rate consumer debt is debt consolidation. For instance, you can borrow against the equity in your house by taking a secured loan called a home equity line of credit (HELOC) and pay off all your credit cards with that loan. Many Canadians have used this method, and it shows in the balances they owe.

According to the Canadian credit bureau TransUnion, the average consumer debt (excluding mortgages) held by Canadians during the fourth quarter of 2019 was $30,106. That's up significantly from $21,428 during the fourth quarter of 2014. When you break it down for 2019, they found that those with credit cards had an average balance of $4,326. However, for those with lines of credit, the average balance was

$35,070. The logical conclusion is that many Canadians are using their lines of credit to pay off their credit cards.

Reducing the overall interest rate on your debt by trading credit card debt for a line of credit sounds like a good idea. Trading $10,000 of credit card debt at 20 percent interest for a line of credit at 3 percent is a prudent move. However, if you continue to spend more than you make and run up the credit card debt again, the end result is worse. You end up with twice the debt — $20,000 — half at the lower rate and half at the higher.

The use of lines of credit is also being fuelled by the current ultra-low interest rates. People think, "Why pay the line of credit down when it's so cheap to carry it?" So the debt doesn't get paid off, and it often increases, as there always seems to be something else to buy. Low rates should be used as an opportunity to pay down balances, not increase them, because more of each payment goes to the principal when interest rates are low. If interest rates rise, however, many people with variable-rate debt (e.g., lines of credit) are going to have a problem. This is especially risky for retired people on a fixed income. So do all you can to avoid this situation by resolving to get rid of as much debt as possible before you retire.

Types of Debt

There are two main types of debt: instalment and revolving. Instalment debt is any debt that requires you to make principal and interest payments. Your mortgage and your car loans are examples of instalment debt. With this type of debt, you are forced to pay off the loan. All you do is maintain the payment schedule and the mortgage or loan will be paid off with the last payment.

Revolving debt allows you to borrow up to a predetermined amount (your credit limit) and requires only minimum payments to cover interest and sometimes a small amount of the principal balance. Your credit cards and interest-only lines of credit are examples. The problem with revolving debt is that since there is no requirement to pay down the principal balance of the loan, many people don't. For example, I have an unsecured line of credit from a major bank, and the minimum monthly payment is currently the greater of 2 percent of the outstanding balance or $50. Of course, as soon as I make the minimum payment, I am free to borrow the same amount up to my credit limit again.

Minimum payments on credit cards are often even lower than that. I'm looking at the disclosure statement for a TD Aeroplan Visa Infinite Card, and the minimum payment is $10 plus any interest and fees (plus any past due amount or any amount that exceeds your credit limit). You can tell how low the minimum payment is by referring to the statement on your credit card bill stating how long it will take to pay off the balance in full. The longest I have seen is "never," because the monthly minimum payment times twelve was lower than the annual fee for the card!

Debt Reduction Methods

Now that we have reviewed various forms of debt, let's look at the options to pay off your debts. There are two main strategies: the snowball method and the avalanche method.

The Snowball Method

With this method, you list your debts, starting with the smallest balance up to the largest. You reduce the payments as much as you can on all other debt besides the smallest one and increase the payments on it so you pay it off as fast as you can. Once your smallest debt gets paid off, you add the amount that was going to pay it off to the next smallest debt. You continue doing this until all your debts are paid off.

The main advantage of this method is psychological. It simply feels great to get rid of a debt, even a small one.

The disadvantage is that, unless the interest rate is highest on your smaller debts, it is better financially to pay off the debts with the highest interest rates first. That is the avalanche method.

The Avalanche Method

With this method, interest costs take priority. You list your debts, starting with the one with the highest interest rate, then the second highest rate, etc. Make the minimum payments on all the other debts and allocate any excess funds to the highest rate debt. Once it is paid off, you allocate the amount that was going towards it to the next highest rate debt.

This method saves you more interest than the snowball method. But if the highest rate debt is large, it will take a long time to pay it off. That can be discouraging, which is the reason many people prefer the snowball method.

Choosing a Method

There is a cool website that allows you to see the effects of different strategies: www.whatsthecost.com. Let's try it out.

Let's say you had three debts as follows:

- $12,000 credit card debt at 20 percent
- $10,000 car loan at 8 percent
- $5,000 line of credit at 3 percent

We'll assume that the minimum monthly payment for the credit card and line of credit is $50 and for the car loan it's $250. We'll also assume you have $850 available each month.

If you were using the avalanche method, you'd prioritize the credit card and make monthly payments of $550 to it while making the minimum payments of $250 on the car loan and $50 on the line of credit. In about twenty-seven months, the credit card balance would be paid off. Next, you would target the car loan at 8 percent. You would pay $800 a month on the car loan and pay if off in about six more months. Finally, the full $850 would go to the line of credit, which would be paid off in about five more months. The total time would be thirty-eight months, and the total interest costs would be $4,466.

If you used the snowball method and prioritized the smallest balance (the line of credit) first, then the car loan, and then the credit card, you would pay an additional $3,622 in interest, and it would take you forty-two months.

However, these solutions will only work if you don't add to the debt. As we discussed at the beginning of this chapter, if you continue to spend more than you make, you won't make any progress. As soon as you pay down a debt, the same one or another one will increase to cover the additional spending.

In some cases, a more extreme solution may be warranted.

A Radical Solution

Financial institutions structure and sell products that work to increase their profits, which is not surprising, as they are in business to make money for their shareholders!

We are forced to pay back our mortgages because, as instalment debt, we must cover interest and principal. But we can take essentially as much time as we want to pay back our high-rate credit card debt, since it is a revolving debt that doesn't require us to pay it down. So we can carry our highest rate debt for as long as we want, but we have no option but to pay down our lowest rate debt.

However, there is one product that reverses this situation. It is a flexible line of credit instead of a mortgage. The Manulife One account (www.manulifeone.ca) is an example of this type of account, and it has been offered in Canada for many years. Other major Canadian banks offer similar products, often referred to as home equity lines of credit.

With this type of account, you don't have a separate mortgage and bank account; you have a combined line of credit that you can use as a chequing account. As soon as your paycheque is deposited in your account, the balance of your line of credit is immediately reduced. When you write a cheque, pay a bill, or pay off your credit card, the balance then goes up again. Interest is charged at the end of each month and is added to the balance owing.

Because this line of credit is secured by your house, the interest rate is low. At the time of writing, the Manulife One base rate was 3.05 percent, 0.6 percent above the banks' prime rate of 2.45 percent. The account has a monthly fee of $16.95 ($9.95 for ages sixty and older). In the right situation, this is an excellent solution, but in the wrong hands it could be a problem. For example, it is not a good option for people who can't control their spending and find it hard to resist the allure of available credit. That results in a balance that keeps rising until it hits the credit limit. The balance is unlikely to ever get paid off, or even paid down. But if you are good with your finances, it can be a way to improve your cash flow and financial situation.

If you currently have revolving high-interest credit card debt and your mortgage payments are preventing you from paying it down, switching to this type of account could free up a large amount of cash to do so.

But be very careful: it is easy to fall into the trap of never paying off the balance.

CHAPTER FIFTEEN

Your Home as a Source of Funds

•

IN CANADA, A HOME IS usually considered to be a good investment. During the ten years that ended in April 2020, house prices in Canada increased by an average 5.5 percent per annum. The following chart shows the average house price increases during that period for specific Canadian cities.

AVERAGE ANNUAL HOUSE PRICE INCREASE APRIL 2010 TO APRIL 2020	
City	Average Annual % Increase
Vancouver	6.2%
Calgary	1.0%
Winnipeg	2.7%
Toronto	8.0%
Montreal	3.9%
Halifax	2.5%
Source: Teranet and National Bank House Price Index	

When it comes to retirement planning, however, your investment in your home is not a liquid investment, i.e., you can't cash in a portion of it to spend. In fact, a house is going to be a drain on your resources for as long as you own it. Think of how much money your mortgage payments take from your account each year and even if you have paid off the mortgage, you're still going to have to pay property taxes, utilities, insurance, repairs and maintenance, etc., for as long as you live there.

Using Your Home to Finance Your Retirement

Having established that your house could be a significant investment, how can you use that investment (if you need to) to help finance your retirement? There are several options.

Sell and Downsize

If your kids have moved out, you probably don't need all the space you required when they lived at home. Depending on where you live and the specific housing market, you could sell your house, pay off any amount left on your mortgage, and buy a smaller house. If it's your principal residence, the added advantage is that you don't have to pay capital gains tax on the sale. This could leave you with a significant amount of extra cash to finance your retirement. Another advantage is it will probably cost less to maintain a smaller house (property taxes, utilities, repairs and maintenance, etc.).

To really take advantage of this strategy, you may need to consider moving to a less expensive neighbourhood or possibly out of your city. This may not appeal to you if it means you have to move away from family and friends, especially at a time when you may need some help. Many retirees aren't willing to do that.

WARNING

Downsizing from a house in one of the big cities like Toronto, Vancouver, or Calgary to a condominium in the same city may not mean significant savings in living costs. If you sell a million-dollar house and

Continued on 155

WARNING Cont.

then buy a $900,000 condominium, you may not be much further ahead because you have to take into consideration the monthly maintenance fees and possible special assessments in the future.

Sell and Rent

If you sell your house and would like to stay in the same city, or even move to another one, another solution is renting. This solution frees up a lot of cash, which you could then invest.

Take In a Tenant

In one of the focus groups for this book, one woman told us that after her husband's death she was unable to maintain the cost of staying in her home alone. She decided to take in a tenant to help cover the costs, and the tenant became a great companion.

This could be a good option for you, but make sure you conduct a thorough background check on all potential tenants before you accept them: the right tenant could become your best friend, but the wrong one could ruin your life.

Take Out a Reverse Mortgage

A reverse mortgage is a financial product that allows you to borrow money against the value of your home without having to sell it. You have several options for how the payment is made to you:

- As a lump sum.
- As an annuity, with a monthly cash payment.
- As a line of credit (similar to a home equity line of credit).
- As a combination, with a smaller lump sum and then a smaller annuity.

You defer payment of the loan until you die, sell the house, or move out of it. Interest charges accrue during the period that you borrow the money; the total of the amount borrowed plus all accrued interest is paid back upon sale of the house.

One of the main advantages to reverse mortgages is that there are no specific minimum income requirements, so even low-income seniors can use them. You also don't have to make any payments on the loan, and as a tax-free source of income they do not affect any income-tested benefits you may be receiving, like Old Age Security or Guaranteed Income Supplement.

However, there are some drawbacks:

- They charge higher interest rates than regular mortgages. The last time I checked, the rate was about 3 percent higher than a traditional mortgage, assuming a five-year term.
- The equity you hold in your home (the difference between the value of your home and the balance owing on the mortgage) will decrease as interest on the reverse mortgage accumulates over the years.
- Upon your death (or your spouse's death, if later than yours), your estate will have to repay the loan and interest in full within a limited time, which may be difficult depending on how long it takes to sell the house and settle your estate. (In Canada, the law states that the loan balance cannot exceed the fair market value of the home.)
- Upon repayment, there will be less money left in your estate to leave to your children and other heirs.
- The associated costs are usually quite high, including:
  — Appraisal fee (estimated at $300 to $400);
  — Independent legal advice required (typically $400 to $700); and
  — Legal, closing, and administrative costs (from $1,795 to $1,995 for a title search, title insurance, and other administrative costs).

There is not a lot of competition, but things have recently improved as there are now two organizations offering reverse mortgages. There is the Canadian Home Income Plan (CHIP) offered by HomeEquity Bank and the Equitable Bank Reverse Mortgage.

Look at a reverse mortgage as a last resort.

Take Out a Home Equity Line of Credit

If you have a decent credit rating, a much cheaper solution is to take out an interest-only home equity line of credit before you retire and use it only if you need it during retirement. Remember to apply for it *before* you retire, as it is much easier to get bank approval when your income is higher and you can prove it by showing them your pay slip, T4, or income tax assessment.

The beauty of this strategy is that it costs you nothing until you withdraw funds. It also has the added advantage of lessening the chances of title fraud because it reduces the amount of equity in your home, so there is less for thieves to borrow against by stealing your identity and registering a fraudulent mortgage.

Before You Retire

At a recent seminar, a retiree gave me a very useful tip. He suggested that it is better to make all major repairs to your home before you retire. After you retire and are on a fixed income, it becomes increasingly difficult to absorb the large cost of repairs. So think about your home before you retire. Does the roof need new shingles? Is there a leak in the basement? Will it need new windows soon?

And give some thought to replacing your furnace. They usually last about twenty years, so if yours is approaching that age, it will need to be replaced soon.

TIP

Another tip about your furnace: if you know it will soon need replacing, get several written quotes from reputable companies for a new furnace (and possibly an air conditioner too) in advance. If you don't, and it breaks down in the middle of winter, you'll be at the mercy of any company you can convince to come and install a new one on short notice before all your pipes freeze.

CHAPTER SIXTEEN

Car Strategy: Lease or Buy?

•

IN CHAPTER TWO, WE SAW that the Clarks bought their car, kept it for eight years, and then bought a new one. This resulted in much higher costs during the four years of car loan payments but significantly lower costs during the last four years they owned the car.

This uneven cash flow makes budgeting more complicated during retirement, when you are on a fixed income. However, there is an option that would make it easier to budget: leasing your car.

When I teach my personal finance course based on my book *Smoke and Mirrors*, I always ask the class how many people lease their car, and often hardly any hands go up, but they include mine. Leasing has a bad reputation, but it should at least be considered.

Leasing: The Basics

With leasing, you are essentially renting a car for a number of years, usually three or four, and then giving it back. Because you are returning it at the end of the lease, you only have to pay for the portion you use during the lease. If you bought the car instead, and financed it over the same number of years as the lease, you would be paying for the whole car.

Obviously, if you buy the car, you own it at the end of the term of three or four years and could then continue to use it without making any more payments. However, when you own, you still have the cost of repairs and maintenance for a car that is aging. If you are lucky enough to have a car that doesn't require many repairs, you have an advantage when you own it. However, you could get stuck with a "lemon" where you'll be constantly paying for repairs when the warranty expires.

How They Determine the Monthly Lease Cost

There are five variables when it comes to leasing. You need to know four of them to calculate the fifth. Here are the five variables:

1. Cost of the car
2. Lease interest rate
3. Term of the lease
4. Residual value
5. Monthly lease cost

The key variable that is important to know before you sign the lease is #4, the residual value. This is usually expressed as a percentage of the cost. For example, on a four-year lease, the residual value may be 45 percent or so. A higher residual value is good because you are being given credit for it when the monthly lease cost is being calculated, so a higher residual value means lower lease payments.

BEWARE OF OPEN-ENDED LEASES

The most important thing to confirm before you lease a car is that it is a closed-ended or walkaway lease. That means that at the end of the term you are not responsible for the fact that the car may be worth less than the estimated residual value.

For example, say you leased a car with a cost of $40,000 and an estimated residual value of $20,000 at the end of a four-year lease, but

Continued on 161

> ## BEWARE OF OPEN-ENDED LEASES cont.
>
> when you return it to the leasing company they determine that it has depreciated (lost value) more than they expected and is now worth only $15,000. If you have an open-ended lease, you will be responsible for paying the $5,000 difference. With a closed-ended or walkaway lease, you are under no obligation to pay the difference because it is the leasing company's problem.

The Complicating Factors of Leasing

There are two issues with leasing that you don't have to worry about with owning a car: charges at the end of the lease for excess kilometres driven and excess wear and tear.

Excess Kilometre Charges

When you sign a lease, the agreement will state how many kilometres a year you are allowed to drive. It's usually around twenty thousand, so during a three-year lease you would be allowed sixty thousand kilometres. If you go over, you'll have to pay the leasing company a set rate per kilometre. In the past I leased a Ford Focus, and the excess kilometre charge was $0.12 per kilometre for any mileage over sixty thousand on a three-year lease.

For some people, the risk of a large excess kilometre charge puts them out of the market for leasing. Taxi drivers, many of whom drive over a hundred thousand kilometres a year, would probably never lease their cars.

If you plan to travel more than twenty thousand kilometres a year during your retirement, leasing is probably not for you. However, many people who have not considered leasing (because they travel a lot during their working years) find that they drive much less during retirement, and that creates a situation where leasing might make sense.

TIP

Note that some leases allow an extra kilometre option credit and will reimburse you if you use fewer than the number of kilometres allowed. This reimbursement rate is usually lower than the rate you pay if you go over. This is rare, but it is worth asking for.

Excess Wear and Tear Charges

In addition to the excess kilometre charge, you'll also have to worry about excess wear and tear charges. This is because at the end of your lease, there will be a lease-ending inspection to determine what costs are needed to get the car back to a condition where they can sell it as a used car. You'll have to pay the costs for any damage, such as paint scratches and dents, new tires if yours are significantly worn, etc. If you are hard on your cars, these costs can be significant. (A friend's son leased a truck and used it in his construction job. His excess wear and tear charges were $7,200!) On the other hand, the Ford Focus I leased had no excess wear and tear charges at the end of the lease.

LUXURY CAR WARNING

The more expensive the car, the higher the wear and tear charges are likely to be. Virtually any repair cost of a luxury car is higher than for a standard car, and that applies to the excess wear and tear charges. That's because consumers expect a luxury car to be in great condition, even if it is coming off a lease.

When Leasing Makes Sense

If you are going to be driving less than twenty thousand kilometres per year and treat your cars reasonably well, leasing during retirement may make sense. It may even make sense before you retire. This is especially true if your cash flow is tight and you have credit card debt with a high interest rate. That is because the added costs you are paying in the early years of buying a car are effectively being financed by the high rate on your credit card debt.

In other words, if you lease a car and therefore have lower monthly payments, the excess cash available could be used to pay down the high-interest credit card balance.

Why Leasing Gets a Bad Rap

I think the problem with leasing is that many people abuse it. Instead of leasing a car they could afford to buy, and therefore driving the same car for less per month, they go out and lease a much more expensive car.

For example, say they could afford to pay $500 a month in loan payments to buy a car, but it would cost only $350 a month to lease the same car. Because they can afford $500 per month, they don't lease that car for $350, they go out and lease a more expensive car for $500 a month. That's not good money management!

The Car Lease versus Buy Analyzer

Since your car strategy has a major impact on your retirement spending, I'd like to introduce a spreadsheet that I first created for my book *Smoke and Mirrors*. Like the other spreadsheets in this book, it is a Microsoft Excel document that you can download from my website at www.tra hair.com or at cpacanada.ca/retirement.

To best illustrate how to use it, I'm going to use it on an actual car I leased, a 2014 Ford Focus. First, go to the "Questions" tab on the spreadsheet and answer the following questions.

General	
What is today's date?	5/21/2020
What is your first and last name?	Dave Test
What car are you proposing to lease or buy?	Ford Focus
What is the highest interest rate on any debt that you have?	5.00%

General	
Lease Option Questions	
What amount are you required to put down as a cash down payment?	$690
What additional amounts are due for fuel charge, licence fee, etc., on delivery?	$217
What is the monthly lease payment (including HST, GST, PST)?	$376
What amount is due for a security deposit on delivery?	$0
What is the term of the lease (in years)?	3
What is the lease interest rate per year?	0.00%
What is the end-of-lease option to purchase amount (residual value)?	$10,835
What is the excess kilometre charge?	$0.12
What is the annual kilometre allowance?	20,000
What is the average number of kilometres you expect to drive annually over the course of the lease?	20,000
Buy Option Questions	
What is the purchase price of the car (including all taxes, delivery, freight)?	$25,776
What amount will you put down on the purchase?	$2,000
What is the annual interest rate on the car loan going to be?	0.9%
How many years will you have the loan?	4
What do you think the car will be worth after 9 years?	$2,500

CAR LEASE VERSUS BUY ANALYZER RESULTS FOR DAVE TEST	
Summary	
Date this analysis was prepared:	5/21/2020
The car you are analyzing is:	Ford Focus
Total kilometres allowed:	60,000
Total kilometres expected:	60,000
Your monthly loan payment (principal & interest) is:	$504
The overall advantage/disadvantage to owning is:	$7,518

Year	2020	2021	2022	2023	2024	2025	2026	2027	2028	Total
Year #	1	2	3	4	5	6	7	8	9	Yr. 1–9
Lease Costs										
Cash down payment	$690	$0	$0	$690	$0	$0	$690	$0	$0	$2,070
Additional amts (fuel, lic., etc.)	$217	$0	$0	$217	$0	$0	$217	$0	$0	$651
Security deposit	$0	$0	$0	$0	$0	$0	$0	$0	$0	$0
Lease payments	$4,512	$4,512	$4,512	$4,512	$4,512	$4,512	$4,512	$4,512	$4,512	$40,608
Repairs and maintenance	$250	$250	$250	$250	$250	$250	$250	$250	$250	$2,250
Excess km charge	$0	$0	$0	$0	$0	$0	$0	$0	$0	$0
Excess wear and tear charge	$0	$0	$200	$0	$0	$200	$0	$0	$200	$600
Total Lease Costs	**$5,669**	**$4,762**	**$4,962**	**$5,669**	**$4,762**	**$4,962**	**$5,669**	**$4,762**	**$4,962**	**$46,179**
Buy Costs										
Down payment	$2,000	$0	$0	$0	$0	$0	$0	$0	$0	$2,000
Principal payments	$5,864	$5,917	$5,970	$6,024	$0	$0	$0	$0	$0	$23,775
Interest payments	$190	$137	$83	$29	$0	$0	$0	$0	$0	$439
Repairs and maintenance	$250	$250	$250	$1,000	$2,000	$2,000	$2,000	$3,000	$3,000	$13,750
Residual value	$0	$0	$0	$0	$0	$0	$0	$0	-$2,500	-$2,500
Total Buy Costs	**$8,304**	**$6,304**	**$6,303**	**$7,053**	**$2,000**	**$2,000**	**$2,000**	**$3,000**	**$500**	**$37,464**

Year	2020	2021	2022	2023	2024	2025	2026	2027	2028	Total
Year #	1	2	3	4	5	6	7	8	9	Yr. 1–9
Excess (savings) required to own	$2,635	$1,542	$1,341	$1,384	-$2,762	-$2,962	-$3,669	-$1,762	-$4,462	-$8,715
Disadvantage/Advantage to Own										
Opening balance excess (savings)	$0	$2,635	$4,309	$5,865	$7,542	$5,157	$2,453	-$1,093	-$2,910	N/A
Interest on balance	$0	$132	$215	$293	$377	$258	$123	-$55	-$146	N/A
Excess (savings) required during year	$2,635	$1,542	$1,341	$1,384	-$2,762	-$2,962	-$3,669	-$1,762	-$4,462	N/A
Closing balance excess (savings)	$2,635	$4,309	$5,865	$7,542	$5,157	$2,453	-$1,093	-$2,910	-$7,518	N/A

In Year 1, the total cost to lease the car was $5,669. The cost to purchase the car during Year 1 was $8,304. It therefore cost $2,635 in extra cash during the first year to own the car.

The program automatically adds an annual interest cost of 5 percent (the rate entered on the "Questions" tab) to that balance during Year 2. That is $132. It then adds the excess cash required to buy during Year 2 of $1,542 so the balance of the excess cost to buy, the "Closing balance excess (savings)" is $4,309 after Year 2.

After Year 3, the balance is up to $5,865. That is how much more it would cost to buy the Focus over three years than it would cost to lease it for the same period.

I will then assume the leased car is returned, and I'll add an estimated $200 excess wear and tear charge but no excess kilometre charge, since I'm assuming we don't go over the sixty thousand limit. I'll then assume another similar car is leased at the same terms as the first car.

After Year 4, the excess costs to own have risen to $7,542. Then the years of payment-free ownership start if the car was purchased. You can see during Years 5 to 9 that the cost to lease the car is higher so the line "Excess (savings) required to own" is negative, and the account gets drawn down.

Note that the repairs and maintenance costs each year are estimated. This is the wild card in the equation because it is difficult to estimate. You can see I've estimated the repairs to cost $1,000 in Year 4, $2,000 in Years 5 to 7, and $3,000 in Years 8 and 9.

At the end of Year 9, assuming we could sell the car for $2,500, the closing balance excess is -$7,518. That means the buy option was the winner by that amount.

However, we need to look beyond the numbers to get a true picture.

How Old Is Your Car?

We have really been comparing apples to oranges. With the lease option you would be driving a car that is a maximum of three years old. With the buy option, your car would be up to nine years old. Besides the benefit of that "new car smell," you'd also be taking advantage of improvements that are being made to cars if you replaced it every few years. For example, newer cars tend to have better safety features like air bag technology, accident avoidance features, and improvements in fuel efficiency.

Warranty

With leasing, your car is usually under warranty at all times. This avoids major repairs that you would have to pay for if you owned the car and were out of the warranty period. This is especially important for luxury cars where large repair costs out of warranty are common.

Repair and Maintenance

As I have said, this is a wild card. I once owned a Ford Taurus wagon that I paid for with a five-year loan and then kept for twelve years. It did not require any huge repairs, but was costly during the final few years. In addition, the air conditioning didn't work too well, and the rear window wiper didn't work at all. You may get lucky like I did, but you may not.

Residual Value

I have estimated that we could sell the Focus for $2,500 after nine years. Would someone pay that for a car with about 180,000 kilometres on it? It's possible, but you'd have to go through the hassle of listing it somewhere and finding a buyer. If you get less than $2,500, the amount of the buy option advantage is reduced by the difference.

Conclusion

Leasing is not bad, it's just more complicated than buying because of things like excess kilometre and wear and tear charges.

However, if you want to keep your cash flow constant and eliminate the hassles and risks of owning your car, it just might make sense.

CHAPTER SEVENTEEN

Planning for Elderly Parents and Inheritance

•

YOU MAY BE LUCKY ENOUGH to be in line for an inheritance from your parents. If you are, there is much that can be done to make the process as smooth as possible. This is important because if you and your parents do not plan ahead, your inheritance may be seriously diminished.

There are many issues that create problems when it comes to inheritances:

- It's difficult to discuss with your parents. No one wants to talk about their own demise, so it's tough to bring the subject up. Even so, at least make sure you have a copy of the will so you know what their plans are.
- The timing is often poor. Hopefully, your last surviving parent lives to a ripe old age of eighty-five or ninety. That probably makes you about sixty or sixty-five and close to, or in, retirement. You have to decide well in advance whether to live your life so you can afford to retire on your own or whether you require an inheritance bailout from your parents to make it work.
- Parents are living longer. It's not unlikely that one of your parents will live a long life. That means they are going to have to spend

quite a bit of money over their retirement years, meaning less to pass on to you.

Taxes on Death

When one parent dies, their assets (including RRSPs and RRIFs) can transfer to the surviving spouse tax-free. But when the last parent dies, they are deemed to have disposed of their assets upon their death. Some items are tax-free (e.g., their principal residence and TFSA), but others will attract tax, including the full value of any remaining RRSP or RRIF. Also, if they have any taxable investments, the difference between the original cost and the current market value has to be reported as a taxable capital gain.

Information to Document

When your parent passes away, it's going to be an extremely emotional time. The last thing you need is the headache of trying to dig up all the financial details of their lives.

Here are the basic things you need to have them document.

Advisors	Yes/No	Contact Information (address/phone number(s)/email)	
Accountant			
Lawyer			
Financial advisor			
Doctor			
Insurance agent			
Documents	Yes/No	Location	
Will			
Power of Attorney over financial affairs			
Power of Attorney over attendant care (end of life decisions, etc.)			

Documents	Yes/No	Location	
Grave plot title deeds			
A list of any property owned (including principal residence and any rentals)			
Financial Information	Yes/No	Account Number	Institution (address/ phone number(s)/email)
RRSP			
RRIF			
TFSA			
Regular investment accounts			
Company pension plan			
Annuity contracts			
Bank accounts			
Life insurance policies			
Mortgages			
Lines of credit			
Credit cards			
Other assets/debts			
Other	Yes/No	Location	
Birth certificates			
Marriage certificate			
Social Insurance Number			
Prior years' tax returns			
Jewellery			

The Estate Planning Record Keeper

To make planning for this difficult time easier, I have created a two-page document called the Estate Planning Record Keeper (see Appendix 2). It is a Microsoft Excel spreadsheet that you can download for free from my website www.trahair.com or at cpacanada.ca/ retirement. It can be printed and filled in, or the information can be entered directly into Excel. Add lines as you see fit, and feel free to pass it on to anyone who may find it useful. An investment of a few hours to fill it in could save many hours and thousands of dollars in lost money for the beneficiaries.

What to Do with Your Inheritance

Your parents' estate will owe any taxes on death, and the executor must be careful to make sure all taxes are paid before distributing the assets to the beneficiaries. So if you receive an inheritance, it will be tax-free to you.

Of course, this can positively impact your financial planning for retirement, and the first thing you should consider doing with your inheritance is to pay off any remaining debt you have, starting with the debt with the highest interest rate.

If you want to pay off your mortgage and are locked into a five-year term, there will be a penalty if you pay the outstanding amount. In many cases, you are limited to paying off only 10 percent or so each year. If you have a line of credit instead of a mortgage, it may be possible to pay the whole debt in one payment.

After paying off debt, consider maxing out your RRSP and TFSA accounts and investing any remainder in a regular investment account.

Summary

It is not a subject we want to think about, but as your parents age, it is important for them to have a plan for the end of their lives and to ensure all their documentation is in place. To help you create this plan, CPA Canada has published the second edition of *A Guide to Financial Decisions: Planning for the End of Life*, which documents all the decisions that have to be made. The guide includes useful information on estate planning, business succession, survivor issues, responsibilities of personal representatives, and all necessary documentation. The guide can be downloaded free of charge at cpacanada.ca/financialliteracy.

No matter how difficult it is, you need to discuss these issues with your parents and encourage them to get professional advice and create the necessary documentation so that their wishes are respected and realized and your inheritance is maintained.

CHAPTER EIGHTEEN

Your Company Pension Plan

•

MANY PEOPLE HAVE TO WORRY about funding their own retirement because they don't work for an organization that has a defined benefit pension plan. These people have to be concerned about saving money and how to invest it. They also need to be aware of what's happening in the world's financial system and its stock markets.

For those people fortunate enough to have a defined benefit pension plan, there may not be as much to be concerned about, but the landscape is changing drastically and, as a result, many pension plans are shifting from a defined benefit to a defined contribution plan.

Types of Pension Plans

Defined Benefit Plans

With a defined benefit (DB) plan, you are guaranteed a certain benefit when you retire that is based on a number of factors including your age, salary, and years of service with the company. Each year, pension actuaries calculate the future benefits that are projected to be paid from the plan and determine the amount that needs to be contributed to the plan to fund the projected payout.

THE PROCRASTINATOR'S GUIDE TO RETIREMENT

You may have to work a certain number of years before you have a permanent right to any retirement benefit under the plan. This is referred to as "vesting." If you leave your job before you fully vest, you won't get full retirement benefits from the plan.

DB plans are still quite common in the public sector. The Office of the Superintendent of Financial Institutions (OSFI) is an independent federal government agency that regulates and supervises more than 400 federally regulated financial institutions and 1,200 pension plans to determine whether they are in sound financial condition and meeting their requirements. According to OSFI, 87 percent of government employees are members of a pension plan, and most of them are DB plans. So if you are a government worker, nurse, teacher, hospital technician, firefighter, or politician and you have a pension plan, it is probably a DB plan.

The private sector is a totally different story. OSFI says that 77 percent of workers in this category have no pension at all. If they do have a plan, chances are it is a defined contribution (DC) plan.

Defined Contribution Plans

With DC plans, the employee makes a contribution to the plan that is matched to some degree by the company. Members are usually asked how they want to invest the money, and at retirement there is a pot of money for them to draw from during their retirement. How big the pot is depends on how well the investments perform. There is no guaranteed payment.

Most private sector companies are switching to this type of plan because they are finding it difficult, due to low interest rates and a volatile stock market, to earn sufficient investment returns to make good on the promised amounts for retired employees required by DB plans. Canadians are also now living a lot longer than they used to, and this is further compounding the problem.

Defined Benefit Plans

Recent Changes

If you have a defined benefit plan, you might have been unpleasantly surprised over the past few years by changes that are not in your favour. These changes are happening because many plans are underfunded. OSFI estimates that 74 percent of federally regulated DB plans were underfunded as of December 2018. This means that most plans have insufficient assets to pay out the pensions they have promised.

The negative implications to you as a plan member are twofold: first, increased contribution rates for current workers, and second, decreased benefits for retirees.

Simply put, to get back to full funding, they need more money coming in and less going out.

How DB Contributions Get Calculated

You make contributions to your plan based on your salary. Since DB plans are designed to work with the CPP, there are usually two contribution rates. One rate is up to the CPP's yearly maximum pensionable earnings amount and the other is for earnings above that amount.

For example, the rates for members of Ontario Municipal Employees Retirement System (OMERS) for normal retirement at age sixty-five are 9.0 percent on earnings up to the YMPE and 14.6 percent on earnings over the CPP limit. The YMPE for 2020 is $58,700. So an employee making $100,000 in 2020 has to make contributions of $11,313, which would be matched by the employer.

The good news is that any contribution you make is tax-deductible.

How to Read Your DB Pension Report

If you are a member of a DB pension plan, you should get an annual report on your pension. It usually includes several sections.

Summary

This usually includes:

- Your normal retirement date (often the last day of the month in which you turn sixty-five).
- Your pension earned to the end of the last calendar year (in dollars starting from age sixty-five).
- Your early retirement date and whether there is a penalty to do so (often the last day of the month in which you turn sixty).
- Your total contributions, plus interest to the end of the last calendar year.
- Your beneficiary (the person who will receive any survivor benefit if you die).

Early Retirement

This section should tell you how many additional years of service you'll need to retire with no penalty. This is usually dependent on your age/service factor, which is your age plus credited service (plus eligible service in some cases; see Qualifying Service below). Many plans have an age/service factor of eighty-five or ninety.

Bridge Benefit

Note that most plans have a bridge benefit, which is an additional amount that is paid if you start to receive your pension before age sixty-five but that is only paid until age sixty-five. That's because DB plans are designed to integrate with the CPP retirement pension that usually begins at age sixty-five. In most cases, the bridge benefit won't stop even if you elect to receive your CPP pension early (you can start as early as age sixty).

Your Pension Calculation

This section will detail how they get the amount of your lifetime pension earned to the end of the last calendar year.

Here is an example. The calculation is based on a factor of 2 percent earned per year of work on the average of your best five years of contributory earnings, which is probably the annual salary you earned in the last five calendar years that you worked. This example is for an average salary of $90,000 where you have worked there for ten years (your credited service).

Lifetime pension including bridge benefit calculation:

= 2% earned x credited service (years) x "best five" earnings

= 0.02 x 10 x $90,000

= $18,000

So if you were eligible to retire before age sixty-five without a penalty, $18,000 is the amount you would receive per year to age sixty-five.

The bridge benefit calculation (see previous section) is a bit more complicated because it has to factor in CPP rates. In this example, we'll use the last five years' average CPP YMPE of $56,440, which is the average for the last five years to 2020.

Bridge benefit at age 65 calculation:

= 0.675% x credited service (years) x lesser of "best five" earnings and the five year average CPP YMPE

= 0.00675 x 10 x $56,440

= $3,809.70

So your lifetime pension payable from 65 would be $14,190.30 ($18,000 – $3,809.70).

Note that these figures are in today's dollars (2020) and don't reflect any activity in the future. It is an estimate of the dollars you would receive starting at age 65 (or before for the bridge benefit). If you continue to work and pay into the plan, you would receive a higher amount.

Qualifying Service

Some plans have two different types of service: credited service and eligible service. You can earn credited service through years of regular contributions or by buying back a leave period.

Eligible service can help you reach an early retirement pension without penalty as it is used in the calculation of the age/service factor. In other words, your credited service gets added to your eligible service to get your qualifying service. Your age plus qualifying service equals your age/service factor (usually eighty-five or ninety).

Eligible service can be any years of service with an employer that is a member of the pension plan that isn't credited service. For example, summer student work or previous service that was refunded when you left a previous employer member of the plan.

Summary of Contributions

This section shows the dollar amount of your contributions to the end of the last calendar year and often the total contributions plus interest. Your employer is matching your contributions, but that amount is usually not displayed.

Note that because you are in a DB plan, there is no correlation between the amount you have paid in and the pension you will get because that amount is based on the calculations shown earlier (which don't use your actual contributions).

Locking In

Your report should also make some kind of statement that your benefits are locked in under your province or territory's Pension Act. This means you can't take the value of your pension plan out if you leave your employer. Other options are usually available, including transfers to locked-in RRSPs.

Defined Contribution Plans

How to Read Your DC Pension Report

If you are a member of a DC plan, your report is simpler because it does not have to deal with estimates of future income. You should get information about:

- Formulas for your required contributions (if applicable) and an explanation of how to select or change a contribution rate (if you must elect a contribution rate within a particular range).
- Formulas for employer contributions.

- Timing of your contributions and employer contributions.
- Treatment of voluntary contributions (if allowed).
- How and when contributions are vested and locked in and an explanation of what these terms mean.
- Statement with amounts deducted by the employer from your pay and other amounts due to the pension fund by your employer.
- Description of how any transfers into the fund will be treated.

When you approach the payout phase of a DC plan, however, things get more complicated. That's because you need to convert your pension to another retirement product, which may include (depending on the current legislation):

- Locked-in retirement account (LIRA)
- Locked-in registered retirement savings plan (Locked-in RRSP)
- Locked-in retirement income fund (LRIF)
- Life income fund (LIF)
- Life annuity contract
- Prescribed registered retirement income fund (RRIF)
- Variable benefit

Your plan administrator should provide you with the options available to you as well as any actions you need to take and their deadlines. They should also inform you of any default options that may be applied if you don't act and the impact that the termination of plan membership will have on each investment option.

CHAPTER NINETEEN

Your Credit Card Strategy

•

IF YOU CARRY A BALANCE on your credit card and therefore pay a high rate of interest to your credit card company, you should look for a card with a lower interest rate. The interest you are paying is likely much greater than any kind of rewards you may get, so if you have one, get rid of your rewards card.

On the other hand, if you pay off the balance every month, it makes sense to look for the rewards card that is going to give you the best rewards for any fee you pay. This is especially true after you have retired and are on a fixed income. Deciding which rewards credit card is best for you is not easy because there are hundreds of cards available.

The Financial Consumer Agency of Canada

One of the resources you can use to help find the card that's right for you is the Financial Consumer Agency of Canada's website at www.canada.ca/en/financial-consumer-agency.html. Look for "Financial tools and calculators" on the home page and then select "Credit Card Comparison Tool."

The tool is very easy to use. You simply answer the following questions:

1. What province or territory do you live in?
2. In which currency would you make most of your transactions?
3. Are you looking for a credit card with a low purchase interest rate? You may be considering this option if you don't pay off your credit card in full each month.
4. What kinds of rewards are you looking for? Choose all that apply.

   - Cash back
   - Travel
   - Groceries
   - Gas
   - General merchandise

5. What is the maximum annual fee that you would be willing to pay for your credit card?
6. What is the maximum purchase interest rate that you would be willing to pay on your credit card?
7. What is the maximum cash advance interest rate that you would be willing to pay on your credit card?
8. What is the maximum balance transfer interest rate that you would be willing to pay on your credit card?
9. Are you looking for a specific bank or credit union? Select your preferences (up to ten institutions).
10. Are you a student?
11. Are you looking for a secured card?

I tried a search for a Canadian-dollar card in Alberta with cash back rewards and no limit on annual fee or interest rate that was not for a student and wasn't a secured card and got thirty-five results.

You can also compare cards side by side by ticking the box to the left of the ones you are interested in and then clicking "Compare two or three results."

But when you actually get into the details, finding the best card can be a very complex task, so I sought help from a person with a lot of experience in this area, Robb Engen, a fee-only financial advisor who writes a monthly column for the *Toronto Star*'s Smart Money section and has an award-winning personal finance blog at www.boomer andecho.com. He has an excellent section on top credit cards that he keeps up-to-date.

Using Your Miles

A common complaint Engen gets from readers is about the fees, taxes, and fuel surcharges they have to pay when they redeem their points for travel. In some cases, the fees and taxes come to an amount that is not much less than it would cost to simply buy a ticket for cash.

Several years ago, when travel was a normal thing, I went online to see what the actual benefit of using Aeroplan miles was. I said I wanted to book a return flight using Aeroplan miles for one adult from Toronto, Canada, to Paris, France, leaving on June 6 and returning two weeks later on June 20 in economy class. I found a direct flight leaving Toronto on June 6 and arriving in Paris the next day. The return trip was a direct flight that left Paris on June 20.

This flight would have cost me 31,000 Aeroplan miles plus $609.86 in taxes, fees, and surcharges broken down as follows:

- Carrier surcharge $476.00
- Canada Domestic/International Airport Improvement Fee $25.00
- Canada Harmonized Sales Tax $3.25
- Canada Domestic/International Air Travel Security Charge $25.91
- France Domestic/International Airport Tax $30.30
- France International Passenger Service Charge $42.80
- France Air Passenger Solidarity Tax $6.60
- Total $609.86

To compare that to the cost of the same flight if I paid cash, I went to Air Canada's website. The total cost of the same flight was $903.79, so the difference between the cost of fees and taxes using Aeroplan and the cost for paying cash was $293.93.

According to the Air Canada website, the base fare for paying cash was $294 and the taxes, fees, and surcharges were $609.79 (a difference of $0.07 from the Aeroplan figure). Using 31,000 Aeroplan miles saved me $294. That's about $0.009 per mile, or less than 1 cent.

Another problem with using many rewards cards is the possibility that you won't find a flight on the day you want or that you'll end up having to make a connection or even two that can add hours to your travel time.

Other Ways to Redeem Aeroplan Miles

One of the other ways to use Aeroplan points is for vacation packages. For example, you can redeem reward miles to pay for a portion of Air Canada vacations or cruises. The Aeroplan website says you can get a $1,000 credit for 100,000 miles. That is a benefit of $0.01 per mile, a little more than the Paris flight example. But the key point is that it is easier to use because you don't have to worry about booking a flight on your specific travel day, although apparently the award is applied only after travel is completed.

The other option to use your Aeroplan points is to redeem them for merchandise. For example, a recent search showed a Nikon D5600 camera kit including an 18–55mm NIKKOR f/3.5-5.6G VR lens costs 153,000 Aeroplan miles. The same camera kit on Amazon.ca costs $829. If I add 13 percent HST, the total cost comes to $936.77. That is a benefit of only $0.006 per mile.

HOW YOU EARN AEROPLAN MILES

To earn miles with a TD Aeroplan Visa Infinite Card, for example, you accumulate 1.5 miles for every dollar you spend on your card on purchases at grocery stores, gas stations, drugstores, and online purchases at www.aircanada.com (excluding Air Canada vacation packages). You earn 1 mile for every dollar you spend on all other purchases. You also

Continued on pg 186

---

earn miles twice when you pay with your card and present your Aeroplan membership card at participating retailers and over 170 online retailers through Aeroplan's eStore.

Of course, you can earn miles for flights you book on Air Canada at various rates. Until February 28, 2015, Aeroplan members got 250 miles for flights with a distance flown of up to 249 miles and the actual amount of miles flown for flights of 250 miles or more. It now seems to be determined by a complex matrix that depends on whether the flights are within Canada, between Canada and the US, between Canada and "sun destinations" (Caribbean, Mexico, and Central America), or between Canada and international destinations. It also depends on what class you book (business class, premium economy, latitude, comfort, flex, standard, and economy basic).

Other Travel Rewards Cards

When choosing a rewards card, in addition to the rate of return on your spending, you'll also need to consider annual fees and any sign-up bonuses. The competition for your business is intense, and many premium credit cards are constantly offering enticing sign-up bonuses and sometimes offers to waive the annual fee in the first year. The card that suits you best depends on how you like to travel and where you spend the most money.

Another great source of information about credit rewards cards is at www.ratehub.ca. Here are their top three travel rewards cards for frequent flyers.

TD First Class Travel Visa Infinite

This card has an annual fee of $120, which is currently waived for the first year. You earn 9 TD points per $1 of travel booked online through the ExpediaforTD website and 3 TD points per $1 on your everyday purchases. At the time of writing, this card offered a sign-up bonus of

20,000 TD points (up to $100) after you make your first purchase on the card. You also get a 15,000-point boost each month (within your first three months) if you spend at least $1,000 — up to 45,000 points. This card requires an income of $60,000.

BMO World Elite MasterCard

This card has an annual fee of $150, which is also currently waived for the first year. You earn 3 BMO Rewards points per $1 on travel, dining, and entertainment purchases. You earn 2 points per $1 on everything else. At the time of writing, this card offered a sign-up bonus of up to 35,000 points (value up to $250). You also get VIP lounge access with the included Mastercard Airport Experiences membership, plus four complimentary passes per year ($140 value). This card requires an income of $60,000.

MBNA Rewards World Elite MasterCard

This card has an annual fee of $120. Currently it offers 20,000 bonus points ($200 in travel value) after you make $2,000 or more in eligible purchases within the first ninety days of your account opening. It also offers 10,000 bonus points ($100 in travel value) once you enroll for paperless e-statements within the first ninety days. You earn 2 points for every $1 in eligible purchases, and you redeem points for travel, cash back, brand-name merchandise, gift cards from participating retailers, and charitable donations. This card requires personal annual income of $80,000 or household income of $150,000 or more.

Cash Back Cards

Since we are now dealing with COVID-19, many people are not doing much travelling. If this is your situation, it may be simpler to use a cash back card. All the major banks and credit card issuers offer cash back credit cards with a range of rewards and benefits. These cards are available either with or without an annual fee. Which option is best for you depends on how much you use the card each month and what you buy with it.

You need to know the details of your spending habits before choosing the best one because there are different reward levels for various types of spending.

Top Cash Back Cards

Ratehub.ca has a great online calculator to help you choose at www. ratehub.ca/credit-cards/cardfinder/rewards. Let's try it out. I'll make the following assumptions:

- Credit score: 725–759
- Annual income: $80,000+
- Average monthly spending: $3,000–$4,999
- Monthly spending:
  - Grocery stores $800
  - Gas stations $200
  - Restaurants $650
  - Drug & pharmacy $300
  - Entertainment $300
  - Travel $300
  - Recurring bills $700
  - Other spending $750

Engen ranked the top three cards as follows.

SimplyCash Preferred Card from American Express
This card has an annual fee of $99 and offers 5 percent cash back on all eligible purchases (up to $300) for the first six months and 2 percent cash back when the welcome rate ends. There is no limit to the amount of cash back you can earn.

Using my previous assumptions, the cash earned back would be $1,041 in the first year and $861 per year thereafter.

TIP

Before you sign up for this card, check that the retailers you use will accept American Express.

Tangerine Money-Back Credit Card

This card has no annual fee, and you earn 2 percent Money-Back Rewards on purchases in two Money-Back Categories of your choice and 0.5 percent Money-Back Rewards on all other purchases. Money-Back Rewards are earned automatically and paid monthly, and they can either be applied towards your credit card balance or redeemed into your savings account. There is no limit on the amount of rewards you can earn, and you can change your 2 percent Money-Back Categories to suit your spending patterns.

Using my previous assumptions, the cash earned back would be $1,006 in the first year and $627 per year thereafter.

TD Cash Back Visa Infinite Card

This card has an annual fee of $120, and you earn 6 percent on all purchases for the first three months up to a total of $2,000. Currently, for the first year there is no annual fee for the primary and first additional cardholder.

You earn 3 percent in Cash Back Dollars on eligible grocery and gas purchases and on regularly recurring bill payments set up on your account. You earn 1 percent in Cash Back Dollars on all other purchases made with your card. You redeem your Cash Back Dollars to help pay down your account balance whenever you please (minimum amount of $25).

Using my previous assumptions, the cash back earned would be $968 in the first year and $768 per year thereafter.

Conclusion

In retirement, every dollar is going to count, so optimizing your credit card strategy is vital.

As we discussed at the beginning of this book, tracking your personal spending is the most important thing you can do to help plan for retirement. It also enables you to choose the best credit card because you need to know how much you spend in the various categories in order to determine which card is the best option for you.

So resolve to spend some time researching the available credit card options, and remember that offers are constantly changing, so make sure you use current research results before you switch to a different credit card.

CHAPTER TWENTY

The Financial Implications of Separation and Divorce

•

SEPARATION OR DIVORCE IS OFTEN devastating, both emotionally and financially. The laws in Canada regarding the financial implications of ending your relationship with your spouse depend on where you live, whether you are married or in a common-law relationship, and (if you are married) whether you are separating or getting a divorce.

Separation occurs when two people who have been living together decide to live separately and are not likely to live together again. For married people, separation does not end the marriage.

Divorce is the legal ending of a marriage by a court.

When you separate or divorce, you'll need to address issues including who will keep the marital home (if you decide to keep it), who will take care of the children, who will pay specific expenses, how much spousal or child support will be paid, if any, and how all your property will be divided. It is a stressful time, with many life-altering decisions to be made, including major financial ones.

Getting Professional Help

There are several resources to help you and your former partner reach agreement on these issues. If you can't reach an agreement, the final step is to go to court and have a judge decide, but that will take a long time and is usually very expensive. It makes sense to exhaust all other options before handing the problem over to the courts.

Lawyers

It is important for both of you to hire your own lawyer (or notary if you live in Quebec) who specializes in family law. If you can't afford a lawyer, you may be eligible for legal aid for advice on certain issues through your provincial or territorial governments.

The federal Department of Justice has links to family law information centres across the country at justice.gc.ca/eng/fl-df/fjs-sjf/index.html, or search for "family justice services."

Collaborative Practice

This is an out-of-court resolution process for separating and divorcing couples. It emphasizes full disclosure, respect, and open communication and is good for spouses seeking an alternative to traditional court-based approaches. It is a good process for people who have children together and want to maintain the best possible family relationships over time. If this is available in your area, you and your spouse hire a trained collaborative family lawyer and, if needed, collaboratively trained neutral family and financial professionals. Adding these people does not necessarily mean added cost because the goal is to distribute the work between professionals in a coordinated manner.

The objective is to work together in a cooperative and non-adversarial manner to come to a mutually satisfactory solution in as little time as possible. And that can save you a lot of money.

To find a collaborative practice lawyer in your area, search the Internet for "collaborative practice" and the name of your town or region.

Mediators

If you can't decide on how to divide your property and other financial matters, hiring a mediator is another option. A mediator is a neutral third party who can assist in coming to a mutually agreeable solution. They do not impose decisions on you, so for this to work you and your former partner must be willing to negotiate and compromise.

Arbitrators

Another option is an arbitrator. An arbitrator is similar to a mediator, except that their decision is binding on both you and your former spouse or partner.

Financial Advice

While legal advice is essential, it may also make sense to hire a financial planner or advisor with experience in family breakups. This is especially important if you have a complex situation because the financial and tax implications of separation or divorce escalate when there is a lot of property at stake.

Credit Counselling

Many credit counselling agencies offer support programs that are free of charge even if you don't become a client of their main service (a debt management program).

The Separation Agreement

In most cases, the final outcome of the discussions is a written separation agreement that covers details such as living arrangements, custody and access to the children, how property and any debt will be divided, and any spousal and child support payments.

Separating Your Finances

As soon as you separate or divorce, it is important that you also separate your finances from your former spouse or partner. Open your own chequing account and get your own credit card. Update any direct deposit banking information with your employer, the government, and any other payments you receive to make sure they get into the right account.

Joint Accounts and Loans

You'll have to agree on what to do with any joint assets or debts that you shared with your former partner. Think about joint chequing accounts, credit cards, and lines of credit and make sure to tell your bank what is going on.

A lot of problems can occur if joint accounts are left open. If you don't close these accounts, both of you may continue to be legally entitled to the funds in any joint accounts, as well as being responsible for repaying any debts even if your separation agreement states that only one person is responsible.

If you have a joint loan, for example, the lender can demand that any borrower listed in the loan agreement continue to make the regular payments or even repay the entire amount.

For certain credit cards, secondary cardholders can be held responsible for any balances owing even if they did not sign the original credit card application.

WARNING

If you have been using a secondary credit card in your previous spouse's name, this could potentially be a major problem for you. Because it was not in your name, your use of that card was not building up your credit history.

Your Credit Report and Score

Since you will now be on your own, your credit report and score are going to be very important. Without a good score, you will not be able to get your own credit card or borrow from a bank, and landlords will usually check your credit history before deciding to rent you an apartment.

If you apply for a credit card online and you are declined, you'll know you have a low credit score and need to take immediate steps to improve it.

THE FINANCIAL IMPLICATIONS OF SEPARATION AND DIVORCE

How to Get Your Free Credit Report

One of the first things to do is to request a free copy of your credit report from both of the credit bureaus in Canada. In each case you should be able to order your copy over the phone, and they are required to mail it to you free of charge. Here are the websites and the phone numbers:

- www.equifax.ca, 1-800-465-7166
- www.transunion.ca, 1-800-663-9980

The Devastating Financial Impact

Put simply, two people can live together for much less than if they live apart. Once you separate or divorce, many costs immediately go up, and some can even double. That is because even if you can afford to keep your house, the other partner has to pay to live somewhere else, and if you both used to share one car, a second car will often be required. Therefore, two of your largest expenses, housing and transportation, will immediately increase.

Imagine a couple who each made good money while they were married but who had a lot of credit card debt, a significant mortgage, and also two children to support; i.e., they had constantly spent more than they made. After a divorce, it will be even more difficult for them to live separately and make ends meet. In many cases, there is no alternative but to sell the house and split the proceeds.

Conclusion

There are no easy answers when a marriage breaks up. Besides being one of the most emotionally devastating events a person can endure, the financial implications range from bad to catastrophic. It is important that you and your ex-spouse or partner try to come to a mutual decision without creating huge lawyers' bills, so there will be more money for you and your children to live on. This is especially true when a marriage breaks up when both parties are close to retirement.

How to Track Your Spending

•

BEFORE WE HAD ONLINE BANKING, in order to track your spending you had to manually list all transactions from your personal chequing accounts and credit cards.

Now, instead of entering each of your personal expenses in a spreadsheet, you can simply download a list of transactions from your financial institution. The most common format is a CSV (comma-separated value) file. These records then appear in Microsoft Excel in separate cells. The fewer bank accounts and credit cards you have, the easier this will be. My family has one main bank account and one joint personal credit card. That means I only have to download and manipulate data from two sources.

If you have multiple bank accounts and credit cards, do yourself a favour and get rid of as many of them as you can.

Here is how you can track your spending.

1. Sign In to Online Banking
2. Download the CSV File
Here is a sample of what you may see when you open your CSV file in Microsoft Excel:

	A	B	C
1	DATE	NAME	AMOUNT
2	03-Jan-20	PEDRO'S EATERY	60.77
3	13-Jan-20	PARKING AUTHORITY	6.00
4	31-Jan-20	ASIAN CUISINE	72.54
5	03-Feb-20	PROPERTY TAXES	1,200.00
6	15-Feb-20	CDN TIRE STORE	35.03
7	23-Feb-20	ESSO	61.98
8	28-Feb-20	DELTA HOTEL	60.52
9	03-Mar-20	EXPRESS COIFFURES	31.50
10	23-Mar-20	JOE'S RESTAURANT	210.77
11	30-Mar-20	SPA & SALON	94.50
12	03-Apr-20	SHOPPERS DRUG MART	82.44
13	18-Apr-20	BLACK'S PHOTO	45.18
14	28-Apr-20	BLACK'S PHOTO	-22.59

3. Clean Up the Data

Delete all the payment (deposit) amounts because we want to focus on expenses. You can do that by pointing to the line number (line fifteen, in this case) with your mouse and selecting "Edit" and then "Delete" or by right-clicking with your mouse and selecting "Delete."

If there are any credit amounts in a separate column (e.g., "BLACK'S PHOTO" on line 14), move them to the "Amount" column and change them to a negative amount and then delete the existing credit amount.

Then format the numbers. Highlight the "Amount" column (point to the C heading), select "Format" and then "Cells," choose the "Number" category and then two decimals, and tick the box "Use 1000 Separator (,)." Or right-click your mouse and select "Format Cells…," select "Number," etc.

Here is what the cleaned-up data looks like:

	A	B	C	D
1	DATE	NAME	AMOUNT	
2	03-Jan-20	PEDRO'S EATERY	60.77	
3	13-Jan-20	PARKING AUTHORITY	6.00	
4	31-Jan-20	ASIAN CUISINE	72.54	
5	03-Feb-20	PROPERTY TAXES	1,200.00	
6	15-Feb-20	CDN TIRE STORE	35.03	
7	23-Feb-20	ESSO	61.98	
8	28-Feb-20	DELTA HOTEL	60.52	
9	03-Mar-20	EXPRESS COIFFURES	31.50	
10	23-Mar-20	JOE'S RESTAURANT	210.77	
11	30-Mar-20	SPA & SALON	94.50	
12	03-Apr-20	SHOPPERS DRUG MART	82.44	
13	18-Apr-20	BLACK'S PHOTO	45.18	
14	28-Apr-20	BLACK'S PHOTO		22.59
15	3-May-20	PAYMENT THANK YOU		2000

4. Sort by Name

Sort the data by highlighting the whole table from cell A1 to C14 (press "Control" and "A"), selecting "Data" and then "Sort," and choosing to sort by the "Name" column. It will then look like this:

	A	B	C
1	DATE	NAME	AMOUNT
2	31-Jan-20	ASIAN CUISINE	72.54
3	18-Apr-20	BLACK'S PHOTO	45.18
4	28-Apr-20	BLACK'S PHOTO	-22.59
5	15-Feb-20	CDN TIRE STORE	35.03
6	28-Feb-20	DELTA HOTEL	60.52
7	23-Feb-20	ESSO	61.98
8	03-Mar-20	EXPRESS COIFFURES	31.50
9	23-Mar-20	JOE'S RESTAURANT	210.77
10	13-Jan-20	PARKING AUTHORITY	6.00
11	03-Jan-20	PEDRO'S EATERY	60.77
12	03-Feb-20	PROPERTY TAXES	1,200.00
13	03-Apr-20	SHOPPERS DRUG MART	82.44
14	30-Mar-20	SPA & SALON	94.50

5. Insert a Column for Type of Expense

Insert a column to the left of the "Amount" column by pointing to the C above "Amount" and selecting "Insert" and then "Columns" (or right-click your mouse and select "Insert") and title it "TYPE."

Then enter a description for each item. Note that because we sorted by name in the previous step, similar entries are listed together. This makes it a lot easier, as you can enter the type once and simply copy it.

Here is what you should get:

	A	B	C	D
1	DATE	NAME	TYPE	AMOUNT
2	31-Jan-20	ASIAN CUISINE	Restaurants	72.54
3	18-Apr-20	BLACK'S PHOTO	Photo	45.18
4	28-Apr-20	BLACK'S PHOTO	Photo	-22.59
5	15-Feb-20	CDN TIRE STORE	Home repairs	35.03
6	28-Feb-20	DELTA HOTEL	Hotels	60.52
7	23-Feb-20	ESSO	Gas	61.98
8	03-Mar-20	EXPRESS COIFFURES	Salon	31.50
9	23-Mar-20	JOE'S RESTAURANT	Restaurants	210.77
10	13-Jan-20	PARKING AUTHORITY	Parking	6.00
11	03-Jan-20	PEDRO'S EATERY	Restaurants	60.77
12	03-Feb-20	PROPERTY TAXES	Property Taxes	1,200.00
13	03-Apr-20	SHOPPERS DRUG MART	Pharmacy	82.44
14	30-Mar-20	SPA & SALON	Salon	94.50

TIP

Once you have described items once, keep a listing of all your types to the right of where you are working in Excel and simply copy the ones you want rather than retyping them.

6. Sort by Type

Sort the data by highlighting the table from A1 to D14, selecting "Data" and then "Sort," and choosing the "Type" column. Here is what you should get:

	A	B	C	D
1	DATE	NAME	TYPE	AMOUNT
2	23-Feb-20	ESSO	Gas	61.98
3	15-Feb-20	CDN TIRE STORE	Home repairs	35.03
4	28-Feb-20	DELTA HOTEL	Hotels	60.52
5	13-Jan-20	PARKING AUTHORITY	Parking	6.00
6	03-Apr-20	SHOPPERS DRUG MART	Pharmacy	82.44
7	18-Apr-20	BLACK'S PHOTO	Photo	45.18
8	28-Apr-20	BLACK'S PHOTO	Photo	-22.59
9	03-Feb-20	PROPERTY TAXES	Property Taxes	1,200.00
10	31-Jan-20	ASIAN CUISINE	Restaurants	72.54
11	23-Mar-20	JOE'S RESTAURANT	Restaurants	210.77
12	03-Jan-20	PEDRO'S EATERY	Restaurants	60.77
13	03-Mar-20	EXPRESS COIFFURES	Salon	31.50
14	30-Mar-20	SPA & SALON	Salon	94.50

7. Subtotal by Type

The last step will make the data very easy to analyze. Highlight the whole table from A1 to D14, select "Data" and then "Subtotals…," then:

- For "At each change in:" select "Type"
- For "Use function:" select "Sum"
- For "Add subtotal to:" tick only "Amount"

Leave "Replace current subtotals" and "Summary data below" ticked. Here is what you'll see:

	A	B	C	D
1	DATE	NAME	TYPE	AMOUNT
2	23-Feb-20	ESSO	Gas	61.98
3			**Gas Total**	61.98
4	15-Feb-20	CDN TIRE STORE	Home repairs	35.03
5			**Home repairs Total**	35.03
6	28-Feb-20	DELTA HOTEL	Hotels	60.52
7			**Hotels Total**	60.52
8	13-Jan-20	PARKING AUTHORITY	Parking	6.00
9			**Parking Total**	6.00
10	03-Apr-20	SHOPPERS DRUG MART	Pharmacy	82.44
11			**Pharmacy Total**	82.44
12	18-Apr-20	BLACK'S PHOTO	Photo	45.18
13	28-Apr-20	BLACK'S PHOTO	Photo	-22.59
14			**Photo Total**	22.59
15	03-Feb-20	PROPERTY TAXES	Property Taxes	1,200.00
16			**Property Taxes Total**	1,200.00
17	31-Jan-20	ASIAN CUISINE	Restaurants	72.54
18	23-Mar-20	JOE'S RESTAURANT	Restaurants	210.77
19	03-Jan-20	PEDRO'S EATERY	Restaurants	60.77
20			**Restaurants Total**	344.08
21	03-Mar-20	EXPRESS COIFFURES	Salon	31.50
22	30-Mar-20	SPA & SALON	Salon	94.50
23			**Salon Total**	126.00
24			**Grand Total**	1,938.64

8. Condense the Data

Do you see the numbers 1, 2, and 3 at the top left? Click number 2 and you'll condense the amounts to the totals by type and the grand total. This is what it will look like:

	A	B	C	D
1	DATE	NAME	TYPE	AMOUNT
3			Gas Total	61.98
5			Home repairs Total	35.03
7			Hotels Total	60.52
9			Parking Total	6.00
11			Pharmacy Total	82.44
14			Photo Total	22.59
16			Property Taxes Total	1,200.00
20			Restaurants Total	344.08
23			Salon Total	126.00
24			Grand Total	1,938.64

This will be your total spending by type for one of your accounts. If you start with the total data from your personal bank accounts and credit cards, you'll get a comprehensive view, which is the key to gaining control of your finances and planning for your retirement.

Estate Planning
Record Keeper

•

To download this file, go to www.trahair.com or cpacanada.ca/
retirement.

Glossary

•

Amortization period

The length of time it will take to pay off a loan or mortgage, assuming the same interest rate and payment amount over that period. The most common amortization period for a mortgage is twenty-five years. A shorter amortization period will mean increased monthly payments and reduced overall cost of borrowing (less total interest paid).

Annuity

A product sold by life insurance companies where, for a fixed sum payable up front, you will receive a series of payments for a period of time, often for the rest of your life. This is an option during the year you turn seventy-one when you have to convert your RRSP to an RRIF or an annuity.

Capital gain

The difference between the original cost of a stock or other investment and the price you sell it for. Note that in Canada, only 50 percent of a capital gain is taxed. This is called a taxable capital gain.

Compounding
The generation of income on previous income. In other words, interest paid on interest. For example, if you had $10,000 on January 1 earning interest at 6 percent for the year with interest compounding semi-annually (twice per year), you would earn 3 percent for the first six months, so your $10,000 would grow to $10,300, then for the last six months your $10,300 would grow by 3 percent to $10,609. The extra $9 is 3 percent interest on the $300 interest you earned in the first six months.

Conventional mortgage
You usually qualify for a conventional mortgage if your down payment is greater than 20 percent of the purchase price of the property. Mortgage default insurance is not required in this case.

Deemed disposition
When you are considered to have sold a property even if you didn't actually sell it. This usually triggers tax consequences similar to what would have been the case if you had actually sold the property. For example, if you transfer an investment from a regular investment account to a tax-free savings account, you are deemed to have disposed of it, and if the value at the transfer date is higher than the amount you paid for it, you will have to report the taxable capital gain on your tax return.

Dividend yield
A financial ratio that shows how much a company pays out in dividends each year relative to its share price. If there is no change in the value of the stock, the dividend yield is the return on investment of the stock.

Effective annual interest rate (EAIR)
The annual rate of interest you earn in a year after accounting for the effects of compounding. See the definition of compounding above; in that example, the EAIR is 6.09 percent.

Equity

1. An ownership interest in a corporation through common or preferred stock. When people refer to equities, they are referring to stocks.
2. The portion of your house, or other asset, that you own. For example, if you own a house worth $500,000 and you have a $300,000 mortgage, your equity in the house is $200,000.

Guaranteed investment certificate (GIC)

A Canadian investment that offers a guaranteed rate of return over a fixed period of time, usually ranging from one to five years. They are most commonly issued by banks, trust companies, and credit unions. They are low-risk investments that guarantee you will get back the original amount of money you invested. The rates of return are lower than you may get with stocks because of the guarantee of the return of your principal.

High-ratio mortgage

If your down payment is less than 20 percent of the purchase price of the property, you have a high-ratio mortgage, which must be insured against payment default by a mortgage insurer, such as Canada Mortgage and Housing Corporation (CMHC) or a private insurer. Twenty-five years is the longest amortization period you are allowed for a high-ratio mortgage.

Line of credit (LOC)

An agreement between a financial institution and a customer that establishes a maximum loan balance that the customer has access to. A secured line of credit puts up collateral (often a house) against the amount owing so that if the borrower defaults, the lender can take control of the collateral to recover the funds. The rate of interest is lower on a secured line of credit than an unsecured line due to the guarantee.

Marginal tax rate (bracket)

The rate of tax you would pay on an additional dollar of income. The

THE PROCRASTINATOR'S GUIDE TO RETIREMENT

marginal tax rate for an individual will increase as their income rises; the rate depends on your income and the province or territory in which you live. For example, in Ontario in 2020, if your income was between $48,536 and $78,786, your combined federal and provincial marginal tax rate would be 29.65 percent. If you made over $220,000, your marginal tax rate would be 53.53 percent.

Mortgage
A debt instrument secured by the collateral of specified real estate property where the borrower is obligated to pay back the debt within a specified period of time.

Mutual fund
A type of investment made up of a pool of funds collected from many investors for the purpose of investing in securities such as stocks, bonds, money market instruments, and other assets. They are operated by money managers who invest the funds to produce income in the form of capital gains, interest, dividends, etc. All the key facts related to the fund, including costs and rate of return information, are contained in the fund's "Fund Facts" document.

On approved credit (OAC)
OAC is often heard on radio or TV ads where the offer they refer to is only good if you meet their test of your credit-worthiness, which usually includes checking your credit score.

Rate of return
The profit on an investment over a period of time, expressed as a percentage of the original investment. The time period is usually one year, and the rate of return is referred to as the annual return. For example, a $100 investment at the beginning of the year with an annual rate of return of 5 percent would have a value of $105 at the end of the first year.

Registered education savings plan (RESP)

A product for saving for a child's education. Contributions are not tax-deductible, and earnings in the plan accumulate on a tax-deferred basis. There is no annual contribution limit, just a lifetime ceiling of $50,000. The Canada Education Savings Grant (CESG) is a federal government subsidy of up to $500 per year (20 percent of annual contributions of $2,500), and the maximum grant is $7,200 per child.

Registered retirement income fund (RRIF)

You have to convert your RRSP into an RRIF or buy an annuity by December 31 of the year you turn seventy-one. There are minimum withdrawal percentage amounts that you are required to make each year. For example, by December 31 of the year you turn seventy-two, you have to withdraw 5.28 percent of the opening market value of your RRIF as of January 1.

Registered retirement savings plan (RRSP)

A retirement savings product that allows you to contribute up to 18 percent of your prior year's earned income. Contributions are tax-deductible within limits, and all withdrawals are taxable. The contribution limit for 2020 is $27,230 and for 2021 it is $27,830.

Reverse mortgage

A financial product that allows you to borrow money against the value of your home without having to sell it. Interest charges accrue over the time that you borrow the money. The total of the amount borrowed, plus all accrued interest, is paid back upon the sale of the house.

Tax-free savings account (TFSA)

A savings vehicle where contributions are not tax-deductible but earnings accumulated are never taxed. It was introduced in 2009 with an annual contribution limit of $5,000 per person aged eighteen or older. The limit increased to $5,500 per year in 2013 and 2014 and was raised to $10,000 per year in 2015. It was reduced to $5,500 from 2016 to

2018 then increased to $6,000 in 2019 and remained there for 2020. Unused contribution room is carried forward, and the full amount of any withdrawals can be put back into the TFSA in future years.

Acknowledgements

•

I'd like to start by thanking the one person responsible for the creation of this book's first edition, Cairine Wilson, former Vice-President of Corporate Citizenship, CPA Canada. I have written this book because of Cairine's vision to improve financial literacy throughout Canada.

I'd also like to thank the many people who have contributed their wisdom to the content of the book. That list includes Kurt Rosentreter, Warren MacKenzie, Ron Graham, Doug Runchey, and Robb Engen.

I'd also like to thank Deborah Klotz for arranging, conducting, and reporting on the valuable focus groups in the early drafts of this book and the many participants in my personal finance courses over the years who have provided excellent feedback that is an integral part of this book!

I'd also like to thank my literary agent, Hilary McMahon of West-wood Creative Artists, for her exemplary work on my behalf, and Maggie Tyson, former Manager, Editorial Development for CPA Canada, for her excellent editing of the first draft of this book.

And last but not least, I'd like to thank the person who, years ago, gave me the title of this book: Kristina Klausen, founder/CEO of PandaTree. At the time I knew it was a good title, but I hadn't written the book to go with it yet!

About the Author

•

David Trahair, CPA, CA, is a personal finance trainer, speaker, national best-selling author, and prior *CPA Magazine* columnist. His books include:

*Smoke and Mirrors: Financial Myths That Will
Ruin Your Retirement Dreams*

*Enough Bull: How to Retire Well Without the Stock Market,
Mutual Funds, or Even an Investment Advisor*

*Crushing Debt: Why Canadians Should Drop Everything
and Pay Off Debt*

*Cash Cows, Pigs and Jackpots: The Simplest
Personal Finance Strategy Ever*

He is known for his ability to explain the often-confusing world of personal finance in plain English. Canadians appreciate his no-nonsense style and the fact that his views are totally independent because he does not sell any financial products.

He currently operates his own personal finance training firm and offers online webinars and e-learning courses based on his books to organizations including CPA Canada and its provincial accounting bodies in British Columbia, Alberta, Saskatchewan, Manitoba, Nova Scotia, New Brunswick and Newfoundland and Labrador.